SHARPEN YOUR TEAM'S SKILLS IN

DEVELOPING STRATEGY

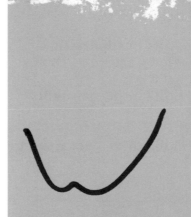

Other titles in this series

Sharpen your skills in motivating people to perform
Trevor Bentley 007 709072 1

Sharpen your team's skills in effective selling
Trevor Bentley   007 709279 1

Sharpen your team's skills in time management
Jane Allan   007 709275 9

Sharpen your team's skills in creativity
Trevor Bentley   007 709282 1

Sharpen your team's skills in coaching
Tony Voss   007 709278 3

Sharpen your team's skills in supervision
Susan Clayton   007 709092 8

Sharpen your team's skills in people skills
Di Kamp   007 709276 7

Sharpen your team's skills in project management
Jean Harris   007 709140 X

SHARPEN YOUR TEAM'S SKILLS IN

DEVELOPING

STRATEGY

Susan Clayton

The McGraw-Hill Companies

London · New York · St Louis · San Francisco · Auckland · Bogotá · Caracas
Lisbon · Madrid · Mexico · Milan · Montreal · New Delhi · Panama · Paris
San Juan · São Paulo · Singapore · Sydney · Tokyo · Toronto

Published by
McGraw-Hill Publishing Company
Shoppenhangers Road, Maidenhead, Berkshire, SL6 2QL, England
Telephone 01628 502500
Facsimile 01628 770224

British Library Cataloguing in Publication Data
Clayton, Susan
  Sharpen your team's skills in developing strategy
  1. Strategic planning
  I. Title   II. Developing strategy
  658.4'012

  ISBN 0-07-709281-3

Library of Congress Cataloging-in-Publication Data
Clayton, Susan
    Sharpen your team's skills in developing strategy.
      p.   cm.–(Sharpen your team's skills)
    Includes bibliographical references (p.   ).
    ISBN 0-07-709281-3 (alk. paper)
    1. Employees–Training of.   2. Work groups.   3. Strategic
  planning.   I. Title.   II. Series.
  HF5549.5.T7C5883   1997
  658.3'124–dc21   96-40933
                                                              CIP

McGraw-Hill

A Division of The McGraw·Hill Companies

Based on an original work by John C Wills, *The ASTD Trainer's Sourcebook: Strategic planning*, 0-07-053442-X McGraw-Hill, New York, 1995

12345 CUP 9987

Typeset by BookEns Ltd, Royston, Herts
Printed and bound in Great Britain at the University Press, Cambridge

Printed on permanent paper in compliance with ISO Standard 9706

To Simon
Whose support and enthusiasm made this possible

CONTENTS

EXERCISES

Series Preface

This series of books focuses on sharpening the performance of your team by providing a range of training and support materials. These materials can be used in a variety of ways to improve the knowledge and skills of your team.

The creation of high performance is achieved by paying attention to three key elements:

- The skills (competencies) of your people
- The way these skills are applied
- The support your people receive from you in applying their skills.

SKILL DEVELOPMENT

The books have been designed so that they can be used as individual workbooks

The books in this series will provide materials for the development of a range of skills on a subject-by-subject basis. Each book will provide information and exercises in manageable chunks (lessons), which will be presented in a format that will allow you to choose the most appropriate way to deliver them to your staff. The contents will consist of all you need to guide your staff to a full understanding of the subject.

There are at least four ways you could choose to guide the learning of your team, these are:

- Training sessions
- Learning groups
- Open learning
- Experiential learning.

TRAINING SESSIONS

These can be run by bringing your people together and guiding them step by step through the materials, including the exercises. During these sessions you can invite your people to interact with you and the materials by asking questions and relating the materials to their current work. The materials will provide you with the detailed information you need to present the subject to your team.

LEARNING GROUPS

This approach involves dividing your team into small groups (two, three or four people) and having a brief session with each group, introducing them to the materials. Each group then works through the materials and meets with you from time to time to assess progress and receive your guidance.

OPEN LEARNING

This approach invites your people to use the materials at their own speed and in their own way. This is a form of individual learning that can be managed by regular meetings between you and your team as individuals or in a group. The process is started by introducing the materials to your team and agreeing some 'learning outcomes' to be achieved.

EXPERIENTIAL LEARNING

This calls for you to invite your team to examine the materials using the exercises as a focus, and then to get them to relate what they are learning directly to real-life situations in the workplace. This experience of learning is then shared and discussed by the team as a whole.

The books in the series have been designed to enable these four approaches to be used, as well as other ways that you might think are more appropriate to your team's specific needs.

APPLYING SKILLS

Time spent developing skills can be wasted if people do not have the opportunity to practise them. It is important that you consider this aspect of performance before embarking on a particular programme. It is useful to be able clearly to identify opportunities for practising skills and to discuss these with your team. Providing opportunities for practising and further developing competency is part and parcel of the whole approach of this series.

PROVIDING SUPPORT

Once people have acquired a new skill and have been provided with opportunities to apply it, they still need your support and coaching while they are experimenting with using it. The opening book in this series, *Sharpen your skills in motivating people to perform*, provides clear guidance on how to help people to develop their skills and then how to provide experience, practice and support as they use these skills.

Before starting work with your team on the materials in this book I suggest you do the following:

1. Review the materials yourself
2. Plan the approach you are going to follow
3. Discuss with your team what you are planning
4. Agree some learning outcomes
5. Indicate how you are going to support your team during the learning process.

You can also make the materials relate to your specific circumstances by doing three things:

- Add local 'colour'
- Adjust the emphasis
- Integrate your own materials.

The authors in the series have endeavoured to provide a range of materials that is comprehensive and will support you and your team. I hope that during this process you learn from and enjoy the experience.

Dr Trevor J. Bentley
Series Editor

ABOUT THE EDITORIAL PANEL

Dr Trevor Bentley, series editor for this series, is a freelance organizational consultant, a facilitator and a writer. Prior to becoming a consultant and while working as a senior executive, Trevor carried out a major research project into decision making and organization structures for which he was awarded his PhD. Over the last 20 years he has had a wide range of experience working with organizations in over 20 countries. Trevor has trained for four years with Gestalt South West and has attended Gestalt workshops in the UK and Europe. He now applies a Gestalt approach in his work.

Trevor has written 20 books and over 250 articles on business related issues. His background includes careers as a management accountant, financial director, computer systems designer, management services manager, human computer interface consultant, trainer and business manager. His current area of interest is in the application of a Gestalt approach to solving problems of organizational harmony. This includes culture change, performance management, team facilitation, executive coaching, mentoring and integrated supervision.

Mike Taylor is a consultant involved in the design, implementation and facilitation of personal and team development programmes within organizations. After graduating in 1987, he worked with two outdoor management training providers, both as a manager and tutor. His work has a strong focus on the use of experiential learning in developing managers, mainly within larger organizations.

Mike also works with groups and single individuals in running meetings and events that help teams and individuals explore working practices and approaches. More recently he has developed an interest in Gestalt as a way of understanding group processes. He is a member of the Association for Management Education and Development.

Dr **Tony Voss** is a counsellor, consultant and trainer. He originally trained as a chemist before working in environmental research developing sea-going computer systems and information technology, and later in the computer industry as a project manager, consultant and quality manager. Tony has a particular interest in enabling people to contribute fully and creatively to their endeavours, and sees this as benefiting individuals, their organizations and society at large. He is an accredited counsellor with the British Association for Counselling, and he has also trained in Gestalt over a four-year period.

Tony works with those wanting to develop their organization and people, and those dealing with particular challenges in their working life. His clients also include those exploring the role of work in their life, as well as those with more personal issues.

ABOUT THE AUTHOR

Susan Clayton, a member of the editorial panel for this series, is a leading contributor to the use and development of Gestalt philosophy and practice in organizations. Focusing on human processes, she enables managers and their staff to achieve business goals that depend on managing people. Her skill in raising awareness of how people relate to each other can forge supportive alliances and powerful cooperative relationships. Her approach includes helping people to manage blocks and difficulties in their contact with others, clearing the way for work and business relationships to move forward and grow.

Susan works with managers at all levels. Her interventions have aided groups in turmoil, managers needing to reach common agreement and individuals needing mentoring and coaching support. She helps organizations understand how to manage in a way that creates trust, respect and clarity in human relationships.

Susan Clayton can be contacted via e-mail at: susan @ feedback.demon.co.uk

CHAPTER 1

ARE YOUR TEAM STRATEGIC THINKERS?

KEY LEARNING POINTS

- Understand different processes in strategic thinking
- Know what type of strategic thinker you are
- Know the range of strategic thinking styles in your team

I remember as a child playing competitive games with friends in nearby woods. We developed strategies to win, we had an idea of what it would be like to beat or capture the other team, we used old tactics that had worked in the past, as well as developing new tricks. We controlled the way we played *and* we came up with new ideas and new strategies. We guessed what might be critical to winning, we were opportunistic and we were uninhibited in our strategic thinking. Like fox cubs learning the skills and tactics to survive through play, we were learning to think strategically through our competitive games. But this learning process was not just about deliberate strategy formation and thinking ahead, it was equally about responding

1

to a changing pattern of events, and building on unfolding ideas as they developed.

Growing up means becoming educated, the educational process often means that we lose sight of strengths which come naturally. Education and learning also leads to behaviours that become habitual; that is, operating through habit rather than considered actions and behaviour. Although this process is essential to our existence as human beings, it can also undermine our potential as strategists.

STRATEGIC THINKING IS ABOUT GIVING UP OLD HABITS

When we talk about strategy invariably people think and speak in terms of:

defining plans based on past experience that will provide a guide to future achievements and successes

This mind set is so strong that people:

1. Do not recognize that there are different ways of forming strategy, even when they think differently themselves.
2. Fail to recognize that thinking strategically is continuous; it is a way of being and learning, not something that you sit down to do through a series of techniques once a year.
3. Treat strategy as an intellectual exercise 'for people at the top'.

When it comes to strategy, much of the time people only see what the mind has been trained to see. Even when they have not been very successful they still go back into old ways of working, old cycles. The fun and creativity in childhood learning has been chipped away by the adult belief system. This mind set is not so much wrong as incredibly limiting – and boring. The challenge is to give up old habits and dead beliefs, allowing our thinking to stretch beyond its current boundaries into new ground.

One such mind set is the belief that strategic thinking is for the managers on the board – the people at the top. But strategic thinking is more than a process operating at board level. Improving the quality of thinking at every level in the organization, and in every aspect of activities, establishes the foundation for daring achievements and leading edge sophistication.

We all have the ability to think strategically and probably use this ability in many ways throughout our lives. Appreciating this is a good starting point for developing your team's skills – you already have a team of strategic thinkers. As their manager your challenge is to bring these skills out and develop them in a way that sharpens your team's ability to formulate strategies – to challenge fixed ways of thinking, to expand the mind and to encourage learning.

The approach taken in this book is that strategy formation is a dynamic process involving both *deterministic* and *emergent* thought processes; both left (logical) and right (intuitive) brain thinking patterns.

> The concept of left- and right-brain thinking patterns is described in more detail in Chapter 4

- In some people left brain activity predominates; in others right brain activity predominates.
- Some people create visions for their future; others respond to opportunities as they come their way.
- Some people plan their holidays right down to the finest detail; others allow their holidays to unfold.
- Some people write their shopping list before they go to the supermarket, and feel lost without one; others carry an intuitive 'list'.
- Some people like to follow a map when they go walking; others like to discover their trail as they go.

Both approaches can be effective unless they become too polarized. Strategic thinking isn't just operating by one or the other style of thinking, it lies in creating a dynamic interplay between these two different thinking patterns.

To help your team gain a good understanding of strategic thinking, this book focuses separately on determined strategy and emergent strategy, before bringing them together in an interplay that will provide each strategist with a powerful and effective way of working.

If you feel the need to swot up on this subject, you could choose to work through the book yourself before developing your team; or, alternatively, you could work with them on an 'emergent' learning process. You can use this book for coaching individuals or for facilitating learning groups, which may be part or all of your team.

To set the learning process off, here is an exercise for both you and your team to do. It will help you become aware of your own style of thinking and the differences within the team.

Exercise 1 – What type of strategic thinker are you?

Place a dot within the space under 'Never' and 'Always' for each question given on the following matrix-type table. When you have answered all the questions, join the dots up. The pattern that emerges will give you some indication as to what type of strategic thinker you are; to the left of the dotted line indicates that you have a preference for 'emergent' thinking, to the right of the dotted line indicates that you have a preference for 'determined' thinking. If your line is balanced equally on both sides then it is likely that you are able to think in both determined and emergent terms equally well.

	Never	Always
1. Are you a person who anticipates what is going to happen in advance?	. . . .	. . . . . .
2. Do you write a detailed shopping list before you go shopping?	. . . .	. . . . . .
3. Are you irritated by people who put forward ideas that seem to carry no rational argument?	. . . .	. . . . . .
4. Do you like to plan your holidays well in advance?	. . . .	. . . . . .
5. Is it important for you to have a clear vision to guide you ahead?	. . . .	. . . . . .
6. Are your books, CDs and music tapes orderly?	. . . .	. . . . . .
7. When assembling new purchases do you read the instructions thoroughly before you start?	. . . .	. . . . . .
8. Do you prefer to work with facts rather than rely on gut feel?	. . . .	. . . . . .
9. Do you prefer to follow a map when you are walking rather than follow a trail and see where it takes you?	. . . .	. . . . . .
	Emergent	Deterministic

The position of your dot will vary slightly according to the circumstances against which the measure is being made. For instance you might prefer to use a map in a foreign country when you are walking, but in this country you like an 'open ramble'. The important thing is that you get a flavour of your preferred style.

Once you have gained a picture of the different thinking styles within your team you can decide how you would like to work through this book. Each part has its own autonomy so you can work through them in a different order.

PART 1 – SETTING THE SCENE

By untangling the complexity of language surrounding strategy and clarifying the terminology as it is used in this book, your team will gain a clear starting point for their learning. They will then go on to discover the importance of working from the heart of the organization as well as through intellect; the relevance of organizational values; and the different conditions that align with different approaches to strategy.

PART 2 – DETERMINED STRATEGY: THE SCIENCE OF STRATEGIC THINKING

This section will help your team learn how to work with *determined strategy*, following the more traditional ways of working from an up to date perspective.

PART 3 – INTRODUCTION TO EMERGENT STRATEGY: THE ART OF STRATEGIC THINKING

Being able to work with *emergent strategy* requires the development of new skills. This section will help your team understand how emergent strategy works and to learn a new set of skills for operating within a new paradigm.

Finally, your team will learn the value of integrated thinking and the importance of bringing into balance with the prevailing conditions these two different aspects of developing strategy.

SUMMARY

We learn to think strategically as children, that is, through both spontaneous and determined thinking. As we get older we are led to believe that successful strategic thinking is based on regularity, logic, consistency and harmony. People who work intuitively, chaotically, with discord and contradiction, have not been recognized or valued for their strategic thinking. Yet the business world today is beginning to acknowledge that success has a great deal to do with contradiction and instability, as well as harmony and consistency.

The skill of the strategist is to value the range of strategic thinking patterns that they see in themselves and in others; to recognize their own preferred styles and the preferred styles of their colleagues; to be able to think strategically in both a determined and emergent way; and to align appropriate thinking patterns with the prevailing conditions.

The emphasis in this book for developing strategy is on the importance of thinking processes in laying the foundations for future actions, and the assumption that strategic planning, where it is deemed necessary, is simply the next logical step.

PART 1

SETTING THE SCENE

Many organizations have grown up on the basis that thought and intellect are the strength of the business. This may be true to an extent, but time has divorced heads from hearts leaving organizations under-performing, oblivious to the fact that the heart has gone from the business. Through a complex web of concepts and language, organizations have attempted to improve performance levels, quality, production and services by working more strategically; that is, through determined strategy. Yet the benefits are short lived when the heart is gone and the web of language for strategy is caught up in a tangled mass of threads.

This section will enable you to untangle the concepts and language of strategy with your team and learn the benefits of working from both the heart and the head. On leaving this section you will have learned about different conditions that interact with different thinking styles.

CHAPTER 2 – WHAT IS STRATEGY: THE CONCEPT, THE LANGUAGE?

This chapter walks you through the maze of language and concepts that surround strategy. By pulling out threads and making clear distinctions, you and your team can make sense of the language to help learning, development and thought. This is like running a piece of coloured string along your tracks through the maze to help you find your way.

CHAPTER 3 – WORKING FROM THE HEART

Here you will explore how to tap into the heart of the organization; of departments, teams and individuals. Your team will apply this learning principle to themselves and their work, understanding how to bring heart and head together to achieve maximum benefit in strategy formation and implementation.

CHAPTER 4 – WAKING YOUR MIND UP

The 'mind gymnasium' offers a series of exercises for stretching your thinking. These exercises will broaden your thinking capacity and increase the suppleness of your mind.

CHAPTER 5 – VALUES

Core values of the business and how they relate to strategic thinking are the focus in this chapter. You will be able to identify the core values of the organization and articulate the team values that will be important to the way you learn the art of strategic thinking.

CHAPTER 6 – THE CONDITIONS

The last chapter in this section illustrates the different strategic approaches that align with different organizational conditions. These conditions mainly refer to the stability of the organization, business and industry. Understanding the relationship between thinking styles and organizational conditions will help you and your team become more 'choiceful' in working strategically.

CHAPTER 2

WHAT IS STRATEGY: THE CONCEPT, THE LANGUAGE?

KEY LEARNING POINTS
- Understand the language surrounding strategic thinking
- Understand the concept of strategy
- Know current approaches towards developing strategy

There is a maze of language surrounding strategy that has developed over decades. This language of interconnected associations shown in Figure 2.1 can be confusing for managers in understanding the concept and the process of strategy. Now, with strategic thinking expanding and stretching beyond the boundaries of linear thought, the strategic journey, the route to business success, is taking on a new language.

For your team to be able to think and act strategically in a way that achieves results, both the concept of strategy and the terminology need to be clear. This chapter explores the language of three specific clusters:

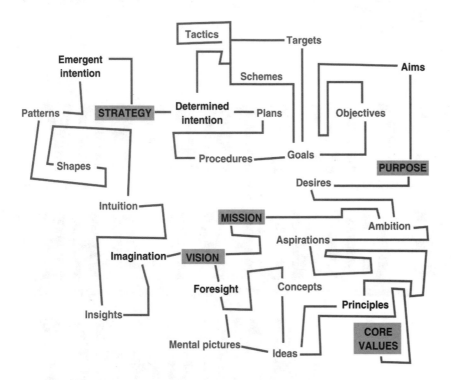

FIGURE 2.1 Strategy as a maze of language

- Strategy – determined and emergent
- Vision
- Purpose – core values and mission.

You will grasp a good understanding of the concepts behind strategy and recognize how the terminology is used in different ways in different situations. You will begin to see that strategic thinking is not a once a year event, but an ongoing pattern of thinking that ranges from the intentional to the responsive.

In the maze shown in Figure 2.1, key words to developing strategy are in shaded boxes with a variety of associated words in black and grey. Throughout the rest of this chapter sections of the maze have been selected, describing in more detail the key word/s, with links made to the associated language.

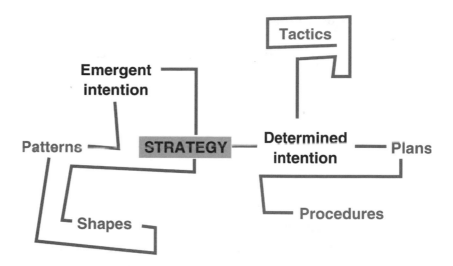

FIGURE 2.2 The maze of language surrounding strategy

STRATEGY

Before we look closely into this cluster let's just review the variety of definitions that people have used to describe 'strategy'.

> **Strategy means control. It is the direction and scope of an organization over the long term, ideally which matches its resources to its changing environment, and in particular its markets, customers or clients so as to meet stakeholder expectations.**
>
> Johnson and Scholes (1988)

> **Strategies are both plans for the future and patterns from the past.**
>
> Mintzberg (1987)

> **The way in which a corporation endeavours to differentiate itself positively from its competitors, using its relative corporate strengths to better satisfy customer needs.**
>
> Ohmae (1982)

> **Plan or course of action leading to the allocation of a firm's scarce resources, over time, to reach identified goals.**
>
> Pascale (1990)

> **The essence of the strategist is managing the conjunction of the political world, or 'polity', with the more day to day routines of tactics and trying to keep them sufficiently in balance without allowing ossification.**
>
> Garrett (1991)

Mintzberg (1987) further defines strategy as walking on two feet, one deliberate, one emergent. That is the approach taken in this book, that developing and implementing strategy is a journey on foot. One foot is the science of strategy, the other foot is the art of strategy; one is deterministic, the other emergent. As they move they change.

It is important that you make a distinction between what is meant by developing strategy in the private sector compared to developing strategy in public services. The efforts of most private businesses are geared towards *making a profit*; to achieving *competitive advantage*. This is not so for the public sector who mainly aspire to *make a difference* and to *seek social change*. This means that strategic thinking processes are similar in both cases, but the content of that thinking is driven by a different set of principles.

The fact that there are so many different definitions can be confusing. You need, therefore, to be clear about *how* you want to work with strategy, individually and collectively, and not get caught up in debates over the semantics of *what* strategy is.

DETERMINED STRATEGY

Determined strategy is the development of logical and intentional steps towards achieving a specific outcome.

Historically, strategy and tactics have been closely linked. They have played a powerful and influential part in the competitive business world and originate from planning approaches in wars.

Determined strategy is traditionally understood as long-term planning, the determined intention to achieve a specific outcome. Tactics are short-term plans which align with the long-term strategy and are very specifically linked to determined strategy.

For example

My strategy for gaining a contract is to meet my client in London rather than Amsterdam; my tactics will be to take the train, rather than drive, so that I can use the train journey to prepare myself for the meeting.

A change in tactics is common when changes in the environment occur. So in the example above, if the trains were delayed I might have to change my tactics in order to re-align myself with the strategy.

Strategy formation has been the process of developing plans, schemes and procedures to establish a direction for action and achieve a predetermined outcome. In the past these plans have held a strong quantitative, analytical function based on shared vision, on shared ideologies. A hierarchical process defines a structure for strategists and for the people who put the strategy in motion.

For example

Vision (or mission)	To give my house a new look
Goals	To re-decorate all the main rooms
Objectives	Complete downstairs rooms by August and upstairs by Christmas
Strategies	Get decorators to do difficult work and do the rest myself in holiday time
	To seek advice on colour coordinates from personal friend who is interior decorator
Action plans	Spend three weeks shopping for new ideas and colour coordinates
	Set out a plan for one room at a time
	Get quotes from decorators

Implementation of plans	
Reviews and controls	Review and adjust timescales/ colour schemes
Rewards	Buy a new lounge suite when completed
	Enjoying the novelty of a newly decorated house

Having a hierarchy does not mean that there exists only one model. Hierarchical structures vary as much as our understanding of the term strategy varies in how different organizational systems use them. The point is that there exists a sequential process which provides a logical order with logical steps – a process that can lead to success. In organizations the business strategy must be accessible for employees to follow and build on in their daily work, otherwise it will be a waste of time.

EMERGENT STRATEGY

Emergent strategy is building on the converging of new and often diverse ideas for the fulfilment of purpose.

Today, strategic management increasingly includes a practice of understanding patterns and shapes of the business; connecting past patterns and future expectations with emerging patterns in the everyday flow of events. The strategic hierarchy is no longer so relevant and strategy formation takes on new shapes.

Incremental actions determined from the strategy are replaced by the converging of collective actions that form the strategy. *Control is different – not absent.*

This movement is not to say that past practices are being thrown out; on the contrary, the linear approach, which in itself has a pattern, still plays a part in strategic thinking. The essence is that different, non-linear patterns now play an important role in developing strategy. These patterns can be

For further reading on emergent strategy you could refer to *Managing Chaos: Dynamic Business Strategies in an Unpredictable World.* Stacey (1992)

understood in terms of an emerging process. This process requires people to be open, flexible and willing to learn. The ideas of different people in an organization converge over time. Strategies grow out of collective action.

A key principle of emergent strategy is learning.

Scenario – Converging ideas

Following a review of employees' competencies through-out the organization, the human resources manager was pondering over an innovative idea for building an infrastructure to support self directed learning, to meet employees' developmental and training needs.

At the same time, a computer technician from the IT department was quietly developing an internal communication system which she felt could offer a useful resource for information exchange within the organization. By chance these two people met one day and happened to comment on their independent projects. Within hours the HR manager had developed a new strategy to support training needs using an Intranet (an internal computer communication system); the IT technician had found an ideal outlet with which to support her initiative.

This is strategy development through an emergent process.

STRATEGY IN CONTEXT

Determined strategy is a useful approach in stable, predictable organizations. Emergent strategy is most appropriate in circumstances where the organization is unstable or too complex to understand. It allows managers to act and respond to the environment before everything is fully understood.

In reality there is no such thing as a purely emergent or purely determined strategy. Either way it would be like attempting a journey relying solely on one leg. On the left leg, it would be impossible to predict the future precisely and avoid learning *en route*, just as it would be ridiculous to rely entirely on the right leg, on a learning process without any sense of control.

This book will help your team to learn how to travel on both 'feet', eventually bringing them together in a dance that adds new dimensions to the strategist's journey.

> In reality there is no such thing as a purely emergent or purely determined strategy

Exercise 2 – Strategists of the past and present

This exercise will help you and your team begin to recognize different strategic styles. A willingness to question and debate will begin to act as useful mind stretchers on your team's thinking patterns.

Write the names from the list below on separate pieces of paper (you could add the names of one or two key people from your organization), then fold up the pieces of paper and put them in a container.

Julius Caesar	Richard Branson
Alice in Wonderland	Big Bird (Sesame Street)
Sir Winston Churchill	Anita Roddick
Napoleon Bonaparte	Bill Gates
Winnie-the-Pooh	Henry VIII

Next, get each member of your team to pick one. Their task is to:

1. Define from what they know so far what they think is the strategic style of the person or character named.
2. Explain why they have come to this conclusion, giving examples.
3. Decide whether the named person's approach was/is successful.
4. State what can be learnt from this person/character in relation to strategic thinking.

Give the team 10 minutes to come up with their answers then allow five minutes each to share these answers in the team, discussing uncertainties and disagreements.

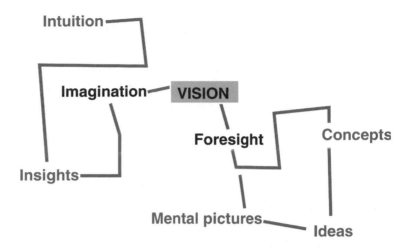

FIGURE 2.3 The maze of language surrounding vision

VISION

A *vision* is commonly known as foresight, a concept or idea, a mental picture of the future, an ideology, as shown in Figure 2.3.

Today it is common knowledge in organizations, and indeed in life, that having a vision of the future creates a tension between what can be achieved and our current reality. The vision sets up a dynamic that otherwise would not exist, making new things possible. Peter Senge (1990) refers to the visioning process as setting up creative tension, where the gap between the future and the present is the source of creative energy. This is like confronting an overgrown garden. Having a vision of what it might look like if the weeds and rubbish were cleared and new plants put in place – with a lawn and paths winding through tree stumps. It is the vision of what is possible that builds the energy source for doing the work.

In the past, an organizational vision used to be very long term – up to 10 years. Today, with rapid change occurring in many organizations, visions tend to be more short term, three to five years. Having vision is not necessarily a means to an end, although it can be; visions are simply a path for future achievements. It is on this path that strategists find their journey.

With the awakening of emergent strategy we can now bring into the visioning process – imagination, insight, intuition and emotional states. These attributes have not been recognized in the past for the value that they bring to strategic thinking. Increasingly we are learning to trust intuition, follow our insights and be more imaginative in our work. Above all, we need to stay in touch with the emotions which are stirred by our vision. These emotions are the tension between the vision and current reality; the driving force that gets us from A to B.

> We need to stay in touch with the emotions that are stirred by our vision

There are some disadvantages in relying on visioning as a process for achieving future successes:

- First, we can never anticipate exactly what events will occur along the way.
- Second, if we rely entirely on the visioning process to take us forward, then we are narrowing our options and inhibiting action. When we create a vision we are basing future expectations on past experiences. This can create a recipe for repetition and an avoidance of innovation.
- Third, in conditions of turbulent change creating a vision can provide management with false comfort; a blanket through which it is easy to ignore the need to learn, to reflect and to respond to current realities.

PURPOSE

Purpose is the passion that drives people and organizations forward (see Figure 2.4).

Having a sense of purpose is becoming one of the most important aspects of organizational development. Often interpreted as a second cousin to the company's mission, and confused with vision, purpose has in the past been under-valued and misunderstood. Where vision creates a picture of a desired outcome, purpose is more abstract. Vision is clearing the overgrown weeds to build a beautiful garden; purpose is the desire to be in touch with nature. A vision with no underlying purpose is an empty dream. Achieving a vision may not fulfil purpose.

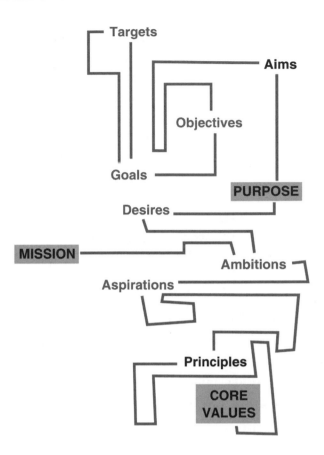

Purpose is at the heart of the business

FIGURE 2.4 The maze of language surrounding purpose

You will discover in Chapter 3 that purpose is at the heart of the business, at the heart of teams and at the heart of the individual. Without purpose there is no heart, there is just head and body, intellect and structure. Even when purpose exists it can still wear a thick cloak of intellect, which focuses on aims and objectives, goals and targets, resulting in a half-hearted attempt to bring life into the work place. Hidden well underneath the cloak are the ambitions of people, their values, aspirations and desires. If you think of yourself and the times that you have given purpose to your work and life, does this affect your motivation and drive? What happens to your motivation when you are asked to do things that are not linked to any purpose?

The passion that drives people forward can be found in

purpose. But rarely do managers and teams take the brave step to lift the cloak and discover the potential of their employees, or to expose their own heartfelt aspirations to the organization. It is not uncommon for groups of managers to discuss the company's purpose and strategy through intellectual discussion. However, intellectual discussions do not necessarily translate into emotional commitment. It is through personal identification with purpose that emotional commitment is found.

Out of purpose grow the organization's values. Purpose and values are rarely explicit, hence the saying 'sense of purpose'.

CORE VALUES

Core values describe how the company intends to carry out its business, what sort of behaviour is ethical, the right way to treat people, and acceptable ways to behave and make decisions. Chapter 5 describes values in greater detail.

MISSION

WHAT IS 'SENSE OF MISSION'?
The term 'mission' tends to lack clarity; it can be, and is, defined and interpreted in many different ways.

In order to understand mission it needs to be separated from vision, with which it is often confused. The word vision conveys a clear meaning of what the organization is aiming for – a picture or mental image of a future state. Mission is more to do with now – the purpose, the business philosophy, the culture. It is about people's values and beliefs, their enthusiasm and pride. Mission is felt emotionally and therefore lies at the heart of the organization and the culture.

Within the mission you can ask a number of questions:

- Why does the company exist?
- What does the company believe in?

- What is distinctive about the company?
- What could the company become?
- What are the behaviour standards that the company subscribes to?

You will visit these questions again in Chapter 11, when your team can look at mission in more depth.

Ultimately the mission has to be conveyed in a simple statement which encompasses all the questions above *and* it has to be understood by management and staff so that they can use it in their daily work.

Exercise 3 – Making sense of the language surrounding strategic thinking

This exercise will help raise your team's awareness of the range and flexibility of the language in strategic thinking and strategy formation. There are no hard and fast rules. The essence is that as a team you hold a common understanding between you in your use and practice of the language.

1. Get your team to find some vision statements, mission statements and aims. They can get these from your organization and others that they are involved with, for example clients, voluntary services, educational institutions. Then test these out against the three clusters described in this chapter. Notice whether the same statement could be used against each cluster through a simple change of words.

For example

An organization in the public sector stated 'Our primary aim is to be a centre of excellence in the provision of …'

This appears to be an aim of the organization because they use 'aim' in the statement. However, it could equally be a mission statement – 'Our mission is to be a centre of excellence'.

Different people work in different ways. The point is that we understand the underlying philosophy, rather than argue whether statements are mission statements, vision statements or aims.

2. This exercise is aimed at bringing out the knowledge and experience that already exists in your team. Discuss with your team their past experience and knowledge of strategic thinking, for instance, other companies where they have worked or educational programmes that they have been on where they have learned theories of strategy.

Has your focus of incremental change been through a process of visioning and strategic planning, or through an emergent process? Can you recognize times when you unknowingly worked with a process of emergent strategy?

SUMMARY

The language and meaning of strategy is evolving, becoming clearer and more flexible with new thinking. Creating a contrast between determined strategy and emergent strategy helps us to understand the confusion of language behind strategic thinking. What matters is the process and choice of actions available to managers – that different processes can be used under different conditions. Managers and teams can expand their options and work with an integrated style of strategic thinking to achieve success, rather than feel constrained by the traditional 'cause and effect' approach.

CHAPTER 3

WORKING FROM THE HEART

KEY LEARNING POINTS
- Understand the sense of purpose that emerges from the heart
- Know how to work from the heart of the organization
- Be able to work from the heart of the team
- Be able to translate purpose into strategy

Tapping into the heart's purpose can be one of the most powerful exercises that any team can engage in towards achieving success. People are driven by heart-felt motives. Yet, over time, organizations have increasingly put more value on left-brain logic than people's emotional contributions in the work place to the point that 'intuition', 'gut feel', driven by a passion' are terms that have not gained respect in many professions and industries. Left-brain logic has been easier to measure and quantify in the intellectual world of business, compared to the qualitative attributes of emotions. So left-brain logic invariably wins over the heart.

Today, in this hugely competitive world, many organizations are looking for different ways of working in order to survive and to take the lead over their competitors. Many are realizing that there may be 'more than meets the eye' to heart-felt contribution which historically has been under-valued. But what does this mean to the strategist and making strategies work?

THE HEART OF THE ORGANIZATION

In truth organizations don't have hearts and emotions, people have hearts, and collectively people carry the heart of the business and profession. At the heart of an organization is a set of values which the employees may or may not subscribe to. When the majority of the people fully subscribe to these values, that is to say there is a good alignment of values, then the organization has a strong heart. People feel good because they can be authentic. Trust and openness germinate and grow easily. People are able to learn and take risks. Creativity and innovation permeate the culture.

Where a lower proportion of people subscribe to the values of the business the organization has a weak heart. Because of misalignments of values employees find their integrity challenged, a protective cover goes over both the heart of the organization and the hearts of the employees. Hearts are central to survival, so self-protection is the first action people will take. There is a closing down of people's potential, of creativity, innovation and the potential of the business.

The open-hearted organization will carry a collective sense of purpose. Many businesses that have appeared to magically become successful overnight can attribute a great deal of their success to an alignment of values and a deep sense of purpose within the culture. The Body Shop is a good example of this. Anita Roddick never set out with a vision of setting up a worldwide business, yet that is what she has achieved through bringing her heart-felt passions into the business – 'running a successful business without losing your soul'.

Your task will be to help your team discover their heart. The following scenario and exercise will help.

My passionate belief is that business can be fun, it can be conducted with love and a powerful force for good. *Body and Soul* Roddick (1992)

Scenario – The restaurant

Caroline and Mark were mother and son. They had taken over the restaurant after Caroline's father died unexpectedly. He had been running it for 15 years and it was the love of his life. His customers came to the restaurant as much to see him as they did to eat. Caroline and Mark were concerned that they would lose customers now that he had gone. They needed to breathe new life into the restaurant. Besides which two new restaurants had started up locally over the past 12 months. This was a small country town; Caroline's father had not had to face this level of competition in his lifetime.

Caroline was prepared to make a go of it, despite the fact that she would have to give up her training to become a nursery nurse. She had hoped to qualify so that she could set up a local pre-school nursery. Caroline invited her son to go into partnership with her since he had a passion for cooking and loved good food. He had recently completed a degree in environmental sciences and was looking for a job.

Exercise 4 – Finding the heart in business

Ask your team:

- What do you think were the very first issues that Caroline and Mark needed to address?
- How could they bring their life interests into the business to give it common purpose?
- On this basis, what chance do you think Caroline and Mark have at making a success of the business?

Imagine you and your team suddenly found yourselves owning a restaurant. Explore the following questions:

- How could the aspirations of individual members of your team be harnessed within the business?
- What would the 'collective' sense of purpose of the business be?

■ Assessing each team member individually, how well aligned would individual aspirations and collective purpose be, on a scale of 1 (low) to 10 (high)?

What does this exercise tell you and your team in relation to your real life work?

AT THE HEART OF TEAMS

Finding the heart in teams is about building good relationships. I hear 'trust' and 'honesty' frequently thrown around as clichés as though they are there to be bargained for. Not at all. Trust and honesty are earned; they come through feeling able to open the heart, to reveal one's vulnerability. In order to do this organizations need to have in place good foundations, defined in Figure 3.1. Without these foundations attempts to develop effective relationships will not work.

Good communication
↓
Mutual respect
↓
Personal safety
↓
Self and environmental support

FIGURE 3.1 Building the foundations for good relationships

To achieve *good communication* and hear the voice at the heart of the team there needs to be *mutual respect* between team members, which includes you, their manager. If mutual respect is poor then trying to build it means reaching down to work at the level of *personal safety* (an individual feeling safe). If personal safety is found to be weak then you need to help people learn how to *support* themselves better and to build effective support networks within the organizational system.

GOOD COMMUNICATION

What do we mean by communication? There are many definitions and many layers that can define good communication in an organization. For now we will refer to the way in which people talk to each other. Good communication at this level lies in the ability to 'engage well' with others, that is, to communicate at a human level, and to take the initiative to change the communication process when contact is low.

Some basic skills for engaging well with others include:

- *Listening* When you or others are not listening well it is worthwhile inquiring as to what is preventing this.
- *Making your conversation clear and concise* Many people waffle on far too much and in so doing lose good contact.
- *Saying what you mean* In risky situations people will wrap up what they want to say in various ways. In so doing they exacerbate the problem rather than take the risk to change it.
- *Making your conversation personal* De-personalizing, like using 'we', 'one', 'they', 'it', 'you' instead of personal 'I' statements can be a clever tactic for self-protection in an unsafe environment, but diminishes your capacity to engage well with others.
- *Seeking clarification* When you seek clarification you indicate to the other person that you are listening and that you need them to expand on what they are saying. This will prevent mis-assumptions or inappropriate expectations later on.

You can usually tell when contact is reduced – people de-personalize, 'switch off', talk in clichés, speak from their role status, intellectualize, seem intent to get their word in and disguise what they really want to say.

MUTUAL RESPECT

These two words are self-explanatory – that there is respect from both, or all, people for each other. Where there is no respect or the respect is one-sided, then communication becomes diminished.

Elements which can get in the way of mutual respect are status, prejudice, lack of self-confidence and self worth, the halo effect, lack of trust, lack of respect for difference and lack of understanding.

Where problems exist that involve you personally, then

somehow you contribute to the problem. Where there is no mutual respect, it is worth exploring what it is that you personally contribute to that problem.

PERSONAL SAFETY

Personal safety is achieved through building an environment where people feel valued for themselves and for their contribution to the team; an environment in which people feel that they can take risks, make mistakes and learn, without the fear of blame and humiliation.

Often through times of rapid change people's personal safety is challenged. The risk of losing jobs, status, power and livelihood attacks people's confidence and self worth. The skills needed to manage these are:

- *Really* listening to and noticing team members and employees.
- Giving spontaneous praise and acknowledgement of good work achieved.
- Valuing others in their differences even when they don't show recognition for you.
- Understanding and owning your own prejudices.
- Taking the risk of openly owning your incompetencies.

When you feel personally safe you begin to open your heart. This leads to mutual respect which leads to deeper communication. Out of this level of communication people are able to gain common purpose.

You will notice that in order to achieve good communication you have to begin it, even at the level of personal safety. This means taking risks.

You must not ignore the impact that mutual respect and personal safety have on an organization, and on the success of business. The contribution teams can make to the business when they communicate well and can truly work from the heart, is too important to ignore.

SUPPORT

Support is a big subject; it means different things to different people and is context dependent. Finding out what support is needed for both individuals and organizational systems means making enquiries. Where support is not adequate it usually entails learning. What this learning is depends on the diagnosis and invariably involves changes in management practices.

Exercise 5 – Finding the heart in your team

Referring back to the idea of the restaurant and that you and your team will be making this business a success, get your team to assess their communication capabilities and agree what could be done to improve this using the matrix type table shown below.

	Things we are already good at	Ways in which we block	How can we improve?
Communication			
Mutual respect			
Personal safety			
Support			

WORKING WITH PURPOSE

It is at this heart level that you can find purpose and commitment; that you will find the passion that drives people forward to succeed. Purpose can get buried underneath power, politics and intellect. I say this because so often I find people acting without purpose; each step is dull and full of effort. On their daily journey they drag their feet until it is time to go home – then their feet wake up.

THE COMPANY'S PURPOSE

Seeking purpose takes us back to the core of our existence, to deeply philosophical questions like 'Why do I exist?'. For a business you must ask 'Why does the company exist?'. In answering the question you discover the 'prime purpose' of the business, the heart of the organization. To reach the heart you may have to sift through a number of layers, as illustrated in Figure 3.2. These layers shift from the obvious to the less visible, where you often have to look and listen a little harder to hear what the heart is saying.

> A vision with no underlying sense of purpose, no calling, is just a good idea. Senge (1990)

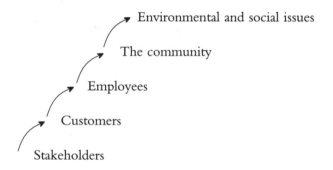

FIGURE 3.2 Organizational layers where purpose exists

Stakeholders will be different in every business, although they generally include people holding positions such as shareholders, board of directors and members, depending on whether the organization is in the public or private sector. The purpose of an organization will be to meet the needs of the stakeholders, for example to maximize the wealth of the shareholders. But life is not that simple; many managers are dissatisfied with this as defining the sole purpose of the business. You have to unveil the complexity of your business systems to find what makes it really succeed, and to understand the power of psychology and motivation in your purpose.

You will then discover different levels of purpose, for

example meeting customer needs and improving customer service, raising standards for employees, supporting the local community and world issues like reaching for a cleaner environment and supporting developing countries. It is often the case that people join an organization because the company carries higher values and seeks a higher purpose than simply supporting the wealth of shareholders or serving the customer. This alignment of purpose between employee and company can be a powerful contributor to business success.

THE TEAM'S PURPOSE

- So, what of the purpose of the team?
- What can your team achieve that team members could not achieve independently?
- What is the real purpose of your meetings?
- Why do you exist as a team?

These are important questions to address and can lead on to discovering common purpose. Out of common purpose comes team spirit, a willingness to learn together, motivation, mutual respect and support, the capacity to achieve high performance.

WHAT IS THE CONNECTION BETWEEN PURPOSE AND STRATEGY?

EXTERNALLY
If the prime purpose is to produce free range eggs from chickens raised in environmentally friendly conditions, the strategy can explain how the company will achieve this. Strategy could define:

Strategy provides the commercial logic for the company.
Stacey (1993)

- The competing market
- The position the company plans to hold in that market
- The competitive advantage that the company has or plans to create.

INTERNALLY
Purpose and strategy need to be converted into company policy and behaviour guidelines that help employees in their

daily tasks. With the above example, if the purpose behind the organization's direction is to produce 'green' eggs from 'green' chickens, then encouraging employees to act within their work on a 'green' basis, setting behavioural standards that support 'green' thinking and 'green' initiatives, enables the organization to act with integrity, for example, in looking for ways in which they can conserve energy. Acting through integrity can have a powerful effect on performance.

Behavioural standards that can help employees integrate the organization's purpose will form part of the business strategy. A word of warning though – building behavioural standards into business strategy without involving and supporting employees to integrate them into their work can lead to cynicism and negative outcomes.

Ultimately, it is a sense of purpose that carries a business forward. Visions come and go, new strategies emerge and fade, but the sense of purpose lives on; the true meaning behind what people do is the life force behind the business.

Exercise 6 – Linking strategy with purpose

On the basis of the 'green egg' company, get your team to make three different suggestions to the directors of the Green Egg Farm on the table provided, translating purpose into strategy for each of the following functions. Production, for example, might need to consider the amount of space allocated 'per chicken'.

	Suggestions
Production	1. 2. 3.
Marketing	1. 2. 3.

Sales	1. 2. 3.
Packaging	1. 2. 3.
Transport and facilities	1. 2. 3.
Finance and administration	1. 2. 3.
Human resources development	1. 2. 3.
Personnel administration	1. 2. 3.

SUMMARY

The heart of the organization offers an essential contribution to strategic thinking. It pumps the life blood around the system, it holds the passion and drive to take initiatives forward, it carries the spirit and the soul of the business. Strategists can no longer rely solely on the brain and intellect to support their strategic thinking; they now need to turn to this life-giving element and understand its importance in strategy formation and implementation . . . and like the human heart, it is vulnerable.

CHAPTER 4

Waking your mind up

To become an effective strategist requires constant practice in strategic thinking. It is a daily discipline, not a resource that can be left dormant in normal times and tapped at will in an emergency.

Ohmae (1982)

KEY LEARNING POINTS

Following the exercises in this chapter your team will:

- Be able to practise mind-stretching exercises and techniques
- Know how to stretch thinking beyond current limited patterns

Strategic thinking implies using the head. Working from the head means using *all* of the brain – left and right brain. So what is the difference? Studies have shown patterns which indicate a left–right dichotomy in the way we think and behave:

Left brain	Right brain
Convergent	Divergent
Explicit	Implicit
Intellectual	Intuitive
Deductive	Imaginative
Rational	Metaphorical
Vertical	Lateral
Discrete	Continuous
Realistic	Impulsive
Directed	Free
Differential	Existential
Sequential	Multiple
Historical	Timeless
Analytical	Holistic
Explicit	Tacit
Objective	Subjective
Successive	Simultaneous

Springer and Deutsch (1981)

Managing more strategically begins with thinking more strategically.
Hanford (1995)

Individual differences capture this dichotomy in millions of different ways. Educational systems in western countries have tended to emphasize left-brain thinking, often neglecting the importance and potential of the right brain. You could say that we have over-developed left-brain capabilities and under-developed right-brain capabilities. It may also be true that through nature or nurture, men and women differ in that many women show a greater predominance of right-brain thinking to men, whereas many men frequently put greater emphasis on intellectual and logical thought. Often these differences carry prejudices, usually due to lack of under-standing and faith in the way that other people think. A highly intellectual thinker, for instance, who does not work intuitively will not put trust in intuitive processes, which can lead to a prejudice against others who do – and of course the same can occur for intuitive people in relation to logical thinkers.

The importance of this is that you should begin to notice individual differences, to be aware of your prejudices, and to draw on the potential in the differences around you. The subject of diversity is discussed in greater depth in Chapter 16.

Second, whatever your make-up it seems that over time we become rigid in our thinking. We lose the elasticity of thought.

In order to deal with rigidity, the mind needs to be 'stretched'. You can do this in a similar way to body stretches, where regular exercise works on the muscle making it become more elastic and in so doing the body becomes more supple and your physical capabilities improve. This chapter will help you work with your team in developing a *supple mind*.

Increasing strategic thinking competencies *is* your job. Garrett (1995)

MIND WORKOUTS

For many, thinking actively does not come easy; we get lazy and do not experiment with new ways of thinking. So we need a *mind gymnasium* where we can turn for regular exercise.

LEFT-BRAIN EXERCISES

The flexible strategist understands the full range of alternatives, constantly weighing the costs and benefits of each one. It is that level of flexibility which increases the chances of success. Considering alternatives requires us to be bold and pose 'what if' questions like 'If the situation was X, what would be the best course of action?', or 'If the situation was Y, could we respond immediately?'

This daily exercise is designed to push the mind into asking 'what if' questions more seriously, and with more regularity.

Exercise 7 – What if . . .

Give this exercise to your managers to do in their own time.

At regular intervals throughout the day, ask yourself a number of different 'what if' questions relating to your career aspirations. Do not answer them, write them down in your day book or diary. You could come back to them at a later date. The essence is that you ask questions that you cannot immediately answer and that you feel challenged by. For instance, you could ask 'What improvements could I make if I understood the architecture of the computer program?', or 'What if I could understand Japanese?'

This technique is a useful tool for the strategic thinker. Encourage your team to develop it to a point of becoming common language in your team.

EXPANDING YOUR KNOWLEDGE BASE

Everything has to do with knowledge – hence strategic thinking!

- Know your product
- Know your industry
- Know your costs
- Know your marketing
- Know your selling
- Know your customers.

Much knowledge and information drifts in and out of your daily life without notice. Often you hold information that you do not share because it seems trivial, irrelevant or unimportant. Yet who are you to judge what others need?

Information sharing is co-created. At times it is more appropriate to ask and to receive; other times it is necessary to give. The strategic thinker cannot afford to let drifting information slip by, however trivial it may seem, nor fail to pass on their own knowledge even though it may seem irrelevant to them. You and your team members are both receptors and providers of knowledge towards the collective wisdom of your team.

You and your team members are both receptors and providers of knowledge towards the collective wisdom of your team

Exercise 8 – Increasing knowledge

From the list above get each member of your team to select a knowledge theme and do the following exercise.

Your task is to find out as much as you can about this particular area in your organization and come back to the team (at the next session) with 10 new things that you have discovered about this area of functioning that you didn't already know. How you do this is up to you. You may wish to use some right-brain exercises (mentioned later in this chapter) to surface ideas of how you could approach the exercise.

In a sense this is an easy task because there are only six kinds of questions that one human being can ask another:

- Why?
- Where?
- When?
- How?
- What?
- Who?

You could draw a mind map of the theme (see the right-brain exercises later in this chapter) using the six words as nodes on the map, as shown in Figure 4.1.

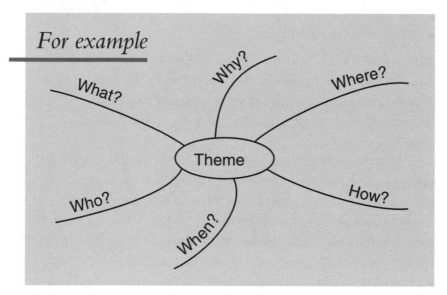

FIGURE 4.1 Increasing your knowledge

At the next session allow time to share and to repeat the exercise, selecting a different theme.

You can repeat this exercise many times, continuously building on the knowledge base of the team.

BUILDING IN NOVELTY

The more you are used to something, the less stimulating it is for your thinking.

For example

Just recently in conversation with a friend I was highly amused to hear his comment in response to a completely absurd and radical idea that I had come up with. He said in a deliberate voice 'This is not beyond the wit of man'. He was somewhat bemused by my laughter until he realized that this saying from Shakespeare was new to me and that the novelty of it had stimulated my amusement.

When thought patterns become disrupted, ideas that create the greatest stimulus to your thinking do so because they force you to make new connections in order to understand the situation. Provocative interventions are often stepping stones that shift a perspective into new directions.

One way of being provocative is by using *manipulative* verbs in thinking, such as: enlarge, reduce, reverse, combine, adapt, eliminate, rearrange, compare, imagine, forge. Notice, for example, how many ideas are based on the verb 'combine' – wine-press, clock-radio, hole-punch, staple-gun, coin-box.

Exercise 9 – Using manipulative verbs

The following is a competitive exercise. Your role as manager will be to keep time and police any ground rules that you decide to bring in before the start. Working in small groups get your team to do the following exercise:

- On a flip chart write up as many manipulative verbs that you can think of in five minutes.
- When time is called, select one word from your list and see how many different ideas you can come up with based on this word in five minutes. Use the example of 'combine' above to generate thinking.

Check with each of the lists to make sure that contents meet the requirements. The winning group is the one with most words.

Another way of stimulating the mind is to interrupt routine activities by:

- Getting to work in a different way
- Using stairs instead of lifts
- Changing working hours.

Engaging in different activities that you normally wouldn't do is another approach. For example:

- Listening to a different radio station
- Trying a different recipe
- Reading different magazines and books.

In other words, bring novelty into your life and push low stimulus routine out. This is a continuous dynamic process of balancing novelty with consistency, for novelty today becomes the routine of tomorrow.

Exercise 10 – Injecting novelty and stimulus into teamwork

With your team look at the routine in your teamwork, habitual behaviours, norms, systems, decision-making processes, assumptions, etc. What is useful and what is deadening? Write up three flip chart sheets and put them on the wall. Get your team to add their own contributions to each of the questions asked.

- What can you bring into your team activities that will increase energy and stimulus?
- What deadening behaviours do your team currently engage in that you could throw out?
- What does your team need to do to sustain a balance between consistency and novelty?

When you have done this, discuss together what steps you will take to change the way you work and sustain the balance.

RIGHT-BRAIN EXERCISES

SYNECTICS
Analogies have been used for many years as an aid to creative

processes. Synectics is a highly developed method which uses metaphor and analogies to generate creative ideas and fresh insights into problems. It is a process that tends to make the familiar strange and the strange familiar.

For example

Use a tin of spaghetti as an analogy of a business. List the attributes of the tin of spaghetti, for example round, made of tin, with nourishment tightly sealed in and a label on the outside, etc. The next step is to force the attributes of the tin of spaghetti to be like the organization, for example the external world sees the hard exterior of management but inside the organization is a rich and nourishing culture.

The exercise frequently exposes attributes from a perspective that hadn't been considered before.

Exercise 11 – Synectics

To practise this exercise for the first time you could get your team to look at themselves as a team through the characteristics of an object.

- Do this by getting a team member to name an object
- Involve the team in identifying the attributes of the object
- Then get them to make connections between these attributes and themselves as a team.

STORY BOARDING

Walt Disney developed the system of story boarding many years ago and today it is a popular management tool used to facilitate creative thinking processes.

When you put ideas up on a story board you begin to see patterns and interconnections: how one idea relates to another and how all the pieces come together. An illustration of this is shown in Figure 4.2. Once the ideas start flowing people start 'hitch-hiking' onto other ideas. Ideas can be generated through *creative thinking sessions* or *critical thinking sessions*. These are structured times purely for ideas generation which are captured on the cards on the story board. Always run these two sessions separately – it could get rather confusing if you ran them together.

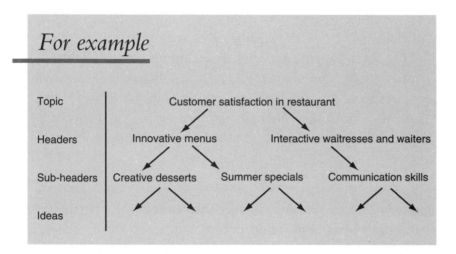

FIGURE 4.2 Story board

The skill lies in thinking positively, holding criticisms back until you have reached an appropriate time for them to be discussed.

There are a number of software programs available that offer story board facilities, but working with cards in group sessions offers a dimension that computers cannot capture. Story boarding can be used for planning, ideas generation, communicating and organization.

Exercise 12 – Story board

For this exercise you will need some A5 card and thick felt pens, a surface to stick card to (large sheets of brown paper will do) and ReMount adhesive.

Decide on a topic or theme and write this on a card. Then

run a five-minute creative thinking session capturing your ideas on more of the cards.

Starting with the topic card build your story board, with header cards containing general points, categories, considerations, etc. Next, under the header cards put sub-header cards containing the ideas that fall under each header; they are detailed ideas generated either in a creative thinking session, or ideas that develop and support the headers as you work together.

MIND MAPS

Our thinking patterns operate through a process of making associations and recognizing links. Association plays a dominant role in nearly every mental function and words themselves are no exception. Every single word we use and idea that surfaces has numerous links attaching it to other ideas and concepts.

Mind maps, developed by Tony Buzan, are an effective method of surfacing links and generating ideas. To make a mind map, you start from the centre of the page with the main idea and work outwards in all directions producing a growing and organized structure composed of key words and key images. An example is shown in Figure 4.3.

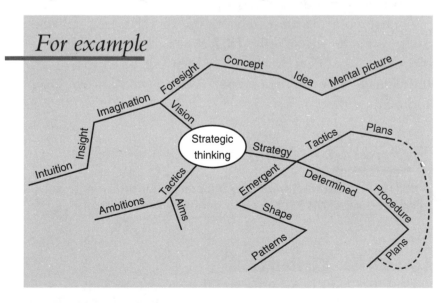

FIGURE 4.3 Mind Map

Key features are:

- Organization
- Key words
- Association
- Clustering
- Visual memory
- Uniqueness
- Conscious involvement.

Mind maps help the development of organization in your thinking process. Once a mind map is drawn up it seldom needs to be referred to again.

Every item in a mind map is in effect a centre of another map.

The creative potential in a mind map is useful in brainstorming sessions. Using the basic problem as the centre, you can generate ideas and associations from it in order to arrive at a large number of different possible approaches.

By using space, colour, shapes, symbols and pictures rather than words, a better overview is gained and new connections can be made visible. Mapping in this way enables you to write your ideas more quickly than expressing them only through words or phrases.

Help your team members to use this approach collectively, for instance on a flip chart when they are working together. This offers more variety than lists of words. Individually they can use computers or the well-known 'paper and pen' method.

Exercise 13 – Mind mapping

A task your team members may choose to undertake is to start a mind map with 'MYSELF' as the central word.

LATERAL THINKING

Granny is sitting painting and three-year-old Sam is upsetting Granny by playing with her brushes. One parent suggests putting Sam in the playpen. The other parent suggests putting Granny in the playpen to protect her from Sam. That's lateral thinking!

Lateral thinking is about thinking sideways when working on a problem to try different perceptions, different concepts, different points of entry. There are two different dimensions to lateral thinking:

■ Systemic techniques for changing concepts and perceptions
■ Exploring multiple possibilities instead of pursuing linear thinking.

The term covers a variety of methods including provocations to get you out of your usual thought processes. Lateral thinking cuts across patterns in a self-organizing system and is influenced by perception.

Exercise 14 – Lateral thinking

1. Ask your team to come up with 30 different uses for a toothpick.
2. There are three restaurant scenarios below, each one carrying a different problem. The task of your team is to come up with 15 different ways for approaching each problem.

> - One of the specialities of the restaurant is their homemade bread. The chef has burnt all the bread rolls half an hour before the evening opening time. The bread rolls normally take two hours to make because they need time to prove.
> - A waitress has spilled red wine over the dress of the bank manager's friend. The bank manager is a good customer of the restaurant and 'provider' of essential loans and overdrafts.
> - A rowdy party of 15 regulars are disturbing the enjoyment of the other 43 customers in the restaurant, who include a group of regional newspaper reporters visiting the restaurant for the first time.

3. In this apparently random row is a hidden word. You can find it by crossing out six letters. To succeed you must use *non-conventional thinking*.

BSAINXLEATNTEARS

You can find the answer in the Appendix.

There are many mind–stretching exercises in circulation. The skill lies in looking for them and building your own mind gymnasium – it costs less than keeping the body fit!

SUMMARY

Skilled strategic thinkers use the full capacity of their minds. They detect things which others fail to see. They search out missing information and do not assume that the knowledge and facts they are given are all that exist. They check out their assumptions and ask the right questions that help them discover 'what it is they don't know ... that they don't know'. They are curious, enquiring and reflective. They balance left-brain logic with right-brain creativity. They always carry the assumption that there is a missing piece of knowledge that will inform them. The capacity of their minds can be stretched beyond their perceived limits – it just requires the discipline of regular exercise.

CHAPTER 5

VALUES

KEY LEARNING POINTS

- Understand the purpose of core values
- Know how to make core values explicit and put them into practice
- Know how 'supporting' values are established

The underlying principles which provide the basis for strategic thinking come from the values held by the organization. These are often referred to as *core values*: they are the basic beliefs held by the organization. A clear set of an organization's core values can serve as a set of ethical principles. The organization's core values define what are and what are not permissible directions managers and teams may take in their strategies. Core values are backed up by *supporting values*.

CORE VALUES

Core values are a way of articulating the heart-felt purpose and aspirations that tap into the organization's (and people's) intended direction. They provide the ground, the earth out of which common purpose and shared vision can be cultivated. They are usually set by the people at the top of the organization, and express *how* an organization will carry out their business.

Examples of core values

- Customer relations are vital to the business.
- We place high value on environmental and social issues.
- Customer satisfaction is our first priority.
- Highly motivated and well trained staff are important to us.

Many organizations have not made their core values explicit; they are embodied in the organization having been built up over a long period of time. In fact, in a family business family values can still be highly influential long after the founder's death. No longer thought about consciously, they exist because they have in the past brought success. People joining an organization are not necessarily told of the core values; they are not made explicit, but are implicit in the way the organization works and people behave. Newcomers are expected to conform to the values, which most of the time they do through a need to be accepted and to belong.

When articulating core values, don't fall into the trap of establishing a set of aspirations or statements that cannot be modelled in practice. People must be able to understand the core values in behavioural terms, to know how to put them into practice and to be able to challenge each other when they are not practised well. Employees need to know what choices are available to them in a range of situations and between competing priorities. Too many core values will become confusing. One or two core values are usually enough.

Core values need to be lived, to have the capacity to be reviewed and changed if they are not right, then to become the bedrock of the organization's culture. Above all, core values need to make sense to the survival of the business. For some companies this will mean questioning whether their deeply held core values prove to be a competitive disadvantage in the marketplace and, if so, how they will continue to

People must be able to understand the core values in behavioural terms, to know how to put them into practice

operate. This issue has been seen over the years in the car industry where some core values have been very strong. For example precision engineering, high quality standards, advanced technology have resulted in some specialist cars to become priced out of the market.

Values play an important part in establishing a vision for the business. The way a vision is developed can reflect the values of the organization. For example, is it the work of a few senior managers, or a subject shared by many because employee involvement in the business is a corporate value?

Exercise 15 – Core values

The Proms
Sir Henry Wood (1869–1944) was an English conductor who founded the Promenade Concerts in London. When he died the BBC committed themselves to carry on his good work and make the Proms a success. Essential to his work was the presentation of the very best of music, especially English music, and making it accessible to students.

1. Ask the music lovers in your team to identify how Sir Henry Wood's values are 'lived' in the Promenade Concerts of today.

The restaurant
2. Imagine you and your team are taking over the restaurant of Caroline's father (described in Chapter 3). Get your team to name three core values that you imagine he would have wanted carried on in the restaurant. Are these values that the team would subscribe to? If not, how would they want to change them *to make a difference to the business*?

Your organization
3. Get your team to name three core values that exist in your organization. What specific behaviours would a visitor or new employee see that would give them a clue as to what the core values of the organization are?

SUPPORTING VALUES
Although not core to the business these are a set of values that

support the core values; that put the nourishment into the ground and the motivation into people. It is here that employees can become involved and add their thoughts and ideas and bring their own values into the system. Their involvement will contribute to a good alignment of organizational values with individual values.

Examples of supporting values

- There is no place for the 'not invented here' syndrome.
- We will seek to build 'environmentally friendly' principles into our work.
- Teams will operate from a clearly defined purpose for working as a team.
- Our responsiveness to customers will be sharpened by a good understanding of what our colleagues are doing.

You will notice that supporting values are about how people work together, so it makes sense that the employees define these themselves, rather than top management doing it. In defining supporting values people get a sense of the boundaries of behaviour; what goes and what doesn't go around here. They commit to values this way far more than 'being told' what values they have to subscribe to.

Exercise 16 – Aligning staff values with organizational values

Get your team to name five values that are important to them in their work as a team. Ask them:

1. How these values connect with the organizational values that they identified in Exercise 15.
2. How these values get 'played out' in their work.
3. How they might challenge each other when individual team members behave in a way that contradicts these values.

SUMMARY

No matter how relevant to vision and strategy the organizational values may be, no matter how clearly they are communicated and discussed, the real test is simple – do they make a difference? Do they substantially influence the day to day behaviour of people at work? The strategist will need to ask questions about the values: their effectiveness, explicitness, how well they express the purpose of the business and ownership of the values by employees.

Values make a difference to developing strategy.

CHAPTER 6

THE CONDITIONS

KEY LEARNING POINTS
- Be able to assess the organizational conditions and decide the most appropriate style for strategy formation
- Understand the relationship between personal style and organizational conditions
- Be able to align your personal style of thinking with opposite styles

Two important dimensions which affect you and your pattern of thought when developing strategy, are:

1. The current state of the organization and business.
2. Your personal style of strategic thinking.

These two dimensions are illustrated in Figure 6.1, with the vertical axis representing the organization and the horizontal axis representing you.

A good awareness of these two dimensions will positively impact on the approach you adopt in relation to determined and emergent strategy, and the outcomes of your thinking. You and your team will plot your position on this chart shortly.

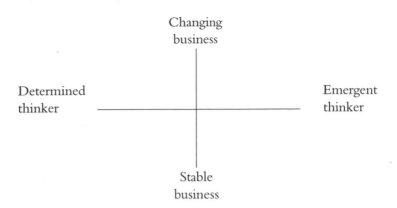

FIGURE 6.1 Linking organizational conditions with personal style

DIFFERENT CONDITIONS MAKE A DIFFERENCE

THE ROLE OF COMPETITION

It is through the world of competition and conflict that the concept of strategy has developed. In the competitive world that we live in today, strategy formation makes a significant contribution to business success. Personal ambitions and aspirations can, of course, also be achieved through strategic thinking, and here again we find we are often up against high levels of competition. Competition drives us, excites us, enables us to learn, challenges us, encourages innovation and pushes us towards achievements, at times far beyond our expectations.

> Competition drives us, excites us, enables us to learn, challenges us, encourages innovation and pushes us towards achievements, at times far beyond our expectations

Strategy, then, defines actions aimed at directly improving the strength of the business, in relation to external competition. Yet the approach that the strategist takes often doesn't work because they do not grasp that, first, different approaches are more successful according to certain conditions relating to stability and change; and second, that preferred styles of thinking influence personal perceptions of these conditions.

STABLE CONDITIONS

In stable conditions an organization will follow exactly the same pattern of behaviour until disturbances promote change.

The culture of a stable organization will be harmonious, strategies consistent, and the organization able to adapt well to the environment. Change is predictable and new developments are dictated by the environment. The success of the organization remains relatively constant and can lead to a view that success is achieved through moving towards a status quo.

In this type of organization determined strategy works well, the future is reasonably predictable and the past can inform the strategist with a reasonable amount of certainty. However, you must question any assumptions which you carry that success is achieved through harmony and consistency. Strategies can become repetitive and over-adapted to their environment. Contradiction and instability can be as successful, if not more successful, than harmony and consistency.

You must also question whether focusing 'in' on the organizational system alone is adequate. With a growing emphasis today on systems thinking, the strategist must also begin to look out to the larger complex system within which their organization functions, that is, the national and international economic and political climate. Small, insignificant changes in this wider system can create major changes for your organization, which is why you need to expand your strategic thinking into new paradigms.

CHANGEABLE CONDITIONS

We are, of course, constantly living in changing conditions. When the situation starts to change rapidly or on a big scale, when the status quo is moved to turbulence through mergers, takeovers, changes in the marketplace, demographic changes, and so on, then we *know* and *feel* change happening. We can say 'we are in changeable conditions'.

When we *know* and *feel* change happening, then we can say we are in changeable conditions

The most significant effect of change is movement in patterns, like continuously twisting a kaleidoscope; we go through a sequence of unpredictable patterns before we settle on one that works. It is the ongoing movement, the unpredictability, that makes determined strategy ineffective in changeable conditions, and leads us towards working with emergent strategy. This can be a problem for the skilled strategist, who understands the changing forces but is being pressurized by the discomforts of others to 'come up with a new strategy to help take the business forward'.

Exercise 17 – Assessment of the conditions of change

The assessment questions given in the table below will enable your team to determine the current internal and external change conditions of your organization. Invite them to do the assessment individually and then to share their responses with each other.

Rate each question by circling the appropriate number on a rating scale, whereby 1 = low, 4 = moderate and 7 = high. There is a space for you to comment on your rating and the impact this could have on your strategic thinking approach.

Assessment question	Rating	Comments
What level of change is your organization currently experiencing?	1 2 3 4 5 6 7	
How much competition does your organization face?	1 2 3 4 5 6 7	
How much does world economy impact on the business you are in?	1 2 3 4 5 6 7	
What level of impact do politics have on the way you work?	1 2 3 4 5 6 7	
How much do changes in the local community affect your business?	1 2 3 4 5 6 7	
What level of change is your industry currently experiencing?	1 2 3 4 5 6 7	
How much competition exists in your industry/profession?	1 2 3 4 5 6 7	
How much pressure exists in your organization to work in a deterministic way?	1 2 3 4 5 6 7	

THE RELATIONSHIP BETWEEN PERSONAL STYLE AND ORGANIZATIONAL CONDITIONS

Because we live in a world of diverse human beings, we also live in a world of diverse thinkers. There is a richness here that you can build on. In Exercise 1 you identified individual preferences in terms of thinking styles in your team. These thinking styles influence how people cope with change, or indeed how they cope with a state of status quo. For example, people who like to work in a determined way, who thrive on structure, will be pulled towards restructuring their environment when widespread change is imposed on them. Alternatively, where an emergent thinker is placed in an environment of little change they will likely seek or create change, for that is what energizes them.

Looking at this phenomenon from the opposite point of view, where people feel at home with the status quo their strategic thinking under stable conditions will flow; where people flourish in change their natural thinking style will be well aligned to changing conditions. In view of these differences people will also perceive change in different ways, which will create a tension in their thinking style.

I imagine that your team will carry a range of styles. The skill lies in building on this at a team level, *valuing* everyone's input to strategy formation however diverse it seems. Such diversity often becomes oppressed in organizations. Your skill as a manager lies in drawing on the richness of the potential that exists in your team in strategic thinking styles. Valuing diverse thinking will be dealt with in more detail in Chapter 15. It is enough for now to know that this potential exists, and to begin to raise awareness of differences in your team through valuing and building on them. The following exercise will help.

Exercise 18 – Raising awareness of diverse thinking

This exercise will help you and your team begin to understand in greater depth different styles of thinking and behaving, and to appreciate these differences. It will be best done outside the group training time and reviewed the next time you are all together.

The holiday

Imagine you are going on holiday with a friend who thinks and operates in a completely opposite way to yourself. How can you work together to get the best out of your holiday in a way that suits you both?

You will gain more by exploring this scenario with someone who carries the 'opposite' characteristics, rather than by making assumptions.

Having identified some of your differences, your first question is likely to be 'What sort of holiday would you choose to have together?' Notice your differences and your discomforts as you explore your holiday. What prejudices do you carry about the other person's different behaviours? Name at least three prejudices that you carry towards your 'opposite style'; if, for example, you believe that intuition is useless in strategic operations, what then is your attitude towards people who work intuitively?

I find when I am working with others that it is not possible to understand all our differences to start with. Often difference emerges through working together. The skill lies in remaining curious to this and surfacing differences fully as they arise.

When you review this exercise with your team you could draw up the two axes in Figure 6.1, at the beginning of this chapter, on a flip chart. Then pinpoint where you believe your organization is and position individually where you and your team are in relation to that point, in your different styles of operating. This will give you a spread of the diversity in your team, and clues where the strengths of your team exist. An example of this is shown in Figure 6.2.

Chapter 16 discusses how to integrate and balance emergent and determined strategy

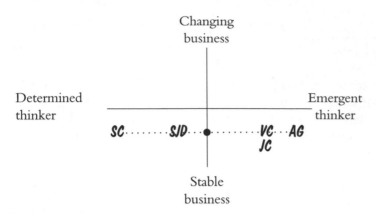

FIGURE 6.2 Linking organizational conditions with personal styles

SUMMARY

There are two dimensions to strategic thinking which you need to align:

1. The strategic process, that is, the balancing of emergent and determined strategy in relation to the level of stability and change currently experienced by the organization.
2. Your personal style aligned with the strategic approach that you decide to adopt.

Holding an awareness of the impact that these two dimensions can have will add value to the outcomes of your thinking and help prevent errors through mis-assumptions.

*D*ETERMINED STRATEGY: THE SCIENCE OF STRATEGIC THINKING

PART 2

STRATEGY AS A SCIENCE

Working with a determined approach presupposes that you have already assessed the state of the organization and concluded a high level of stability within a consistent pattern. You are then able to predict with some certainty the changes in conditions over a given time span, and plan with this in mind. Success is partly dependent on certain assumptions and a good prediction of the future. This cause and effect approach I will refer to as a science, in contrast to emergent strategy which I refer to as an art in Part 3.

PAST, PRESENT AND FUTURE

The six chapters of this section will help you and your team understand the importance of three dimensions in strategic thinking: past, present and future.

CHAPTER 7 – LOOKING BACK

The past informs us about the culture of the organization; how it started, myths and stories that have carried, productive and unproductive ways of working, the effectiveness of systems, where problems lie, where key relationships have influenced behaviour and outcomes over time, the evolution of management and leadership styles, predictable patterns. In other words, what can be learned from the past that can influence future direction.

This chapter will enable you to recognize old unproductive cycles, allowing new ways of working to enter the current paradigm and inform your strategic thinking.

CHAPTER 8 – WHAT'S HAPPENING NOW?

In this chapter you and your team will engage in a well-known technique, a S.W.O.T. analysis, which will help you pull together information relating to the present state of affairs.

A S.W.O.T. analysis offers a way of reviewing the organization's current Strengths, Weaknesses, Opportunities and Threats. This analysis can guide actions that will build on the strengths, avoiding activities when they are weak. You can make the best of opportunities consistent with the strengths and deal with potential threats that might undermine your future plans. This chapter will help you and your team begin to think in terms of these four dimensions.

CHAPTER 9 – KEY FACTORS

Key factors are factors that are important, or even critical, to the success of the business. So the organization must focus energy on these areas.

Your team will learn how to identify success factors and build them into their strategic thinking.

CHAPTER 10 – THE VISION

The ideological approach to strategy formation is generally based on a vision of a future state, an image of what the organization could become if it followed a certain path – a strategic intent. This vision is usually a challenging one; in business it is aimed at winning over competitors. Your team will learn how to create a vision.

CHAPTER 11 – THE MISSION

It is emphasized that not all organizations work with a mission. This chapter explains the purpose and components of a mission, describing how to develop a mission either for your organization or team. It then goes on to help you define the mission in a statement. In working through this chapter, you and your team will discover the benefits of operating from a well-defined mission statement.

CHAPTER 12 – BEYOND THE LIMITS

This chapter offers hands-on skills development through a number of *activities*. In particular it challenges limiting thought processes, presents some interesting questions and raises awareness of the political environment in which you and your team work.

Exercise 19 – *What do you already know?*

Test your team on the depth and breadth of their thinking using the table below. 1 = low; 7 = high.

Question	Rating	How could you improve?	How might you block yourself from improving?
How broad is your view of the organization and industry?	1 2 3 4 5 6 7		
How motivated are you to challenge the status quo?	1 2 3 4 5 6 7		
Do you bring a multi-dimensional approach to problem solving?	1 2 3 4 5 6 7		
To what extent do you understand the politics in your organization?	1 2 3 4 5 6 7		
How good are you at noticing opportunities?	1 2 3 4 5 6 7		
How knowledgeable are you of the factors that lead to success in your business?	1 2 3 4 5 6 7		

CHAPTER 7

LOOKING BACK

KEY LEARNING POINTS

In this chapter you and your team will learn how to reflect on the past and allow this to inform your thinking in the future. Having worked through the exercises you will:

- Understand patterns of the past
- Understand how historical blocks create vicious unproductive cycles
- Be able to chart growth cycles to understand past influences
- Be able to consider in depth the many external influences that impact on the business

UNDERSTANDING THE PAST

Life is lived forward but understood backward. Mintzberg (1987)

To work with a strategic approach that predicts the future you need to understand the past. This information helps you to make certain assumptions about patterns within the business, the industry and within the cultures of the organization and society as a whole. In your reflections you need to:

- Know the myths and stories that are held in the organization. These will give you a clue as to where blocks in the system exist.
- Understand patterns of behaviour in the culture, power

structures, the effectiveness of organizational systems and the stability of the value system of the organization.

■ Understand the pattern of organizational growth and know where you are now in relation to that pattern.

■ Know the performance of the organization against previous plans.

■ Relate the organization's performance to changes in the environment such as demographic changes, increasing competition and fluctuations in the world economy. You need to recognize how the business has adapted predictably to these changes.

■ Have an intimate knowledge of the business.

This information informs you and influences your thinking in the following ways:

■ *Existing* ways of working that are effective can be developed further.

■ *Unproductive* ways of working can be discarded.

■ *New* ways of working can be introduced.

Exercise 20 – Garments of the past

Get your team to do the following exercise together. They can do it in relation to either the organization or to the department.

Head up three sheets of flip chart paper with the headings below. Then ask your team to do this exercise:

Imagine that you have an old antique chest of garments and accessories which symbolize functional and dysfunctional ways of operating in your organization, for example in this chest is a pair of boots and this symbolizes the way management walk around and engage with all members of staff. On each flip chart link garments or accessories with their symbolic meaning in relation to the headings:

■ The garments that you would like to keep and wear more often

■ The garments that you would like to discard

■ Different garments that you would like to introduce (*that you believe would add value to the business*).

Encourage your team to think of behaviours in the culture of the organization as well as operational systems.

STORIES, RITUALS AND SYMBOLS

There is no point in developing new strategies if old patterns of behaviour simply come in and undermine the business, whatever the strategy. It is in the interest of the strategist to recognize the stories, rituals and symbols that are held in the culture of the organization and the implications that underlie them. They hold valuable insights into the core beliefs and assumptions of the organization.

STORIES

Stories, rituals and symbols hold valuable insights into the core beliefs and assumptions of the organization

Stories typically tell of heroes and villains, successes and disasters. They tell what is important in the organization, for example stories of innovation rather than the company's sales achievements immediately give the listener a clue as to what gets rewarded. The behaviour of the key character, of 'macho' behaviour or 'Florence Nightingale', will indicate what is acceptable or not acceptable behaviour. The clues are in both the story that is told and the 'missing story' – what doesn't get into the story books.

RITUALS AND ROUTINES

Every organization will carry routines and rituals. They can give structure and meaning to events. The strategist will need to determine whether they add value to the work of the organization and the richness of the culture. The repetitiveness of rituals and routines can become so automatic that after a while people don't stop to consider their real worth. They may lose their value but continue because of tradition. A typical routine that I frequently question with groups and teams is the way in which people conduct meetings, for example following an agenda can become so embedded in routine that no-one questions its value, despite the regularity of comments like 'that was a waste of time'. These behaviours can either support or hinder the work of the strategist; the skill is in knowing.

SYMBOLS

One of the most important aspects of a culture are the symbols that are carried within it. They inform newcomers and visitors of the types of behaviour that are valued within the organization. They convey messages beyond their functional purpose.

We can find symbols in such things as:

- Language – is it accessible, does it mimic other industries, is it unique?
- Furnishings – are there red carpets and fancy furniture that convey hierarchy, or is the management system invisible within a network of open office space?
- Pictures on the walls.
- What is at the entrance/reception.
- What visitors see and what they don't see.
- Car parking spaces – who has them?
- The building – do staff eat in the same restaurant as management or do restaurants follow the flow of the hierarchy with top management in their luxurious dining room at the top of the building and line workers in the canteen on the bottom floor?
- Clothes – do staff wear uniforms that set them aside from management?
- Public statements – do visible statements indicate the key concerns of stakeholders?

Your task is to assess the value in the message. In most cases the way people behave will be affected. The question is do these behaviours help the growth of the organization? If they are no longer of value, how can they best be changed?

Do the behaviours that culminate from stories, rituals and symbols keep the organization stuck in a vicious, repetitive, unproductive loop, or are they useful in taking the organization forward into virtuous, productive, cycles? Does the organization have the capacity to learn, or do stories, through their very nature, prevent this?

Exercise 21 – Vicious circles or virtuous circles?

This exercise will enable your team to begin to make sense of the obvious – the everyday things that are so easily missed, yet impact on the business.

For example

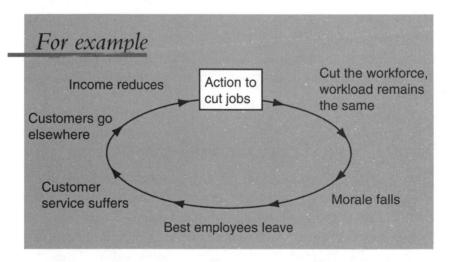

FIGURE 7.1 The vicious circle

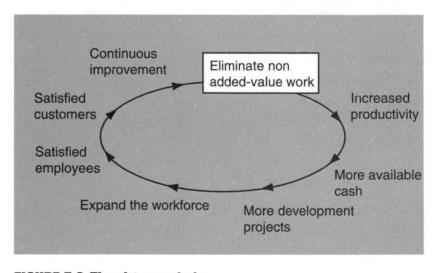

FIGURE 7.2 The virtuous circle

Draw up two flip charts, one with a vicious circle and one with a virtuous circle like those shown in Figures 7.1 and 7.2. Working together with your team:

1. Name 10 symbols (use the list above to help you) in your

organization. Write or draw each one on a card or Post-it note, then stick it on one or the other of the flip charts according to whether it adds to the flow or blocks the flow of organizational functioning.

2. Name three stories that are carried from the past, and on different colour cards or Post-it notes identify up to three consequences of each story, once again positioning them on the appropriate flip chart.

Discuss the outcome of this exercise with your team and the influences that they might need to consider in their strategic thinking.

ORGANIZATIONAL GROWTH

In your thinking you must be aware of where the organization is in its growth cycle. You can only understand this by looking into the past and recognizing growth patterns.

Many mature organizations will have experienced mild to severe discontinuity at times during their growth. There are a variety of causes, some appearing from within and some arising from outside the organization. Typical examples of these are:

- Costs rising
- Returns declining
- New competitors reducing market share
- Customers demanding shorter delivery time frames and new services
- Social values changing, influencing demand for the organization's goods and services.

Such occurrences do not operate in isolation. There are often a number of influences that are interconnected.

For example

In the restaurant scenario two specific occurrences were likely to impact on the growth or decline of the restaurant; first, there was the immediate impact of Caroline's father dying, out of which came the realization of the second issue – growing competition in the area. Caroline and Mark would need to take immediate action to reduce the impact of both of these.

A common problem is for management to leave it too late before they take action to develop new innovations. An attitude of 'when you can see the top of the mountain, start planning the next climb' can be extremely productive. In the science of strategy in the competitive world there is a need to work in parallel with different plans (or new products). Figure 7.3 shows the flow of two plans – there could be many. What happens is that before one upward curve meets its peak, another starts.

However, it would be equally unwise to just leap from action to action. I know many a project that has failed to reach its peak, or important learning has not been gained, due to lack of completion – Plan 2 has caught the interest and so good completion of Plan 1 has failed to occur. There is a lot of overlap between the two plans, as the illustration indicates. The skill is in working with parallel processes.

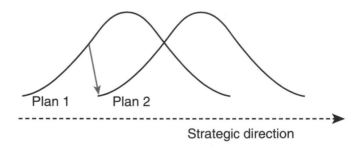

FIGURE 7.3 Planning the next climb while on the 'up'

Exercise 22 – Lifeline of an organization

Show your team the restaurant customer graph in Figure 7.4, reflecting the yearly profit and loss. The numbers relate to the events listed below.

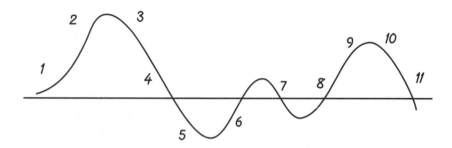

FIGURE 7.4 Restaurant customer graph

The key events to changes in the flow were:

1. Determination and energy of Caroline's father to fulfil lifelong dream.
2. Bought the neighbouring property and extended the restaurant.
3. Father ill, restaurant run by family.
4. Lost three members of staff, difficult to replace.
5. Closed half of the restaurant due to foundations of recently purchased property sinking.
6. Re-opened half restaurant following renovations.
7. Assistant cook went down with salmonella poisoning, closed restaurant as precaution. Discovered that poisoning was contracted elsewhere. Lost customers for a while.
8. Landscaped garden and purchased land down to the river's edge. Opened garden to public for afternoon teas.
9. Opened up new barbecue area in gardens during the summer.
10. BSE scare knocked half the dishes off the menu. People seemed to want more vegetarian dishes which the cook was not knowledgeable about.
11. Father died.

The picture that emerges from this lifeline shows a very different story to the one perceived by Caroline and her family over the years. Caroline's father had always given the impression that 'business was good', despite their setbacks.

Get your team to do the following exercise. You could divide into two small groups, one looking at the organization and one looking at the department.

1. Draw a lifeline of your organization or department showing levels of performance and/or growth curves. Choose a

measure of performance relating to the business that is
important today.
2. Where the curve changes direction on your lifelines, identify
the key influences that impacted on the change.
   – What can you learn from the changes that could influence
     your strategic thinking today?

Really challenge each other on the second question, as it would
be easy to skip through with superficial answers like 'lost three
members of staff because the family were running the restaurant
and didn't manage the staff well'. Although this might be
obvious, there is good learning behind these events such as, *the
family did not attempt to build new relationships with the staff*,
which could give a clue today about how to manage staff in the
future.

LOOKING BACK, LOOKING OUT

It is easy to reflect on the past, to look inward and see
behaviours and the performance of the organization, forget-
ting that the organization has existed within the context of a
much wider system – in the industry, the business world and
the changing needs of customers. The strategist must
remember this and know the type of relationship the business
has had in the past with the outside world and how the
outside world has influenced the business. We reflect here on
the restaurant, but this is a simple example compared to the
complexities of larger businesses. Do not underestimate the
power and influence of the 'less visible relationship' which the
business has with the outside world.

Listed below are the many different facets of the
restaurant and the external relationships which the business
has.

	Contribution
Supplies	*veg, meat, wine/beer/spirits, groceries, etc.*
Staffing	*standard rates of pay, staff relationships, availability of staff in the locality (chef & kitchen staff, waiters & waitresses, bar staff, cleaners, gardener, administrator)*
Finance	*tax, accountants, bank*
Builders/architects	*renovation, materials, themes, style*

Printers	*printing menus, special occasion marketing, printing stationery, quality and competitive rates*
Family	*involvement, support*

Impact

Customers	*needs/demands, community relationships*
Competition	*local trade vs countrywide, business meetings, parties, weddings, variety of food, type of food, etc.*
Politics	*affluence vs pulling in the purse strings*
Weather	*summer barbecues and winter warmers by the fireside, national weather, impact on food supplies*
Society	*changes in food values, media messages*
Local community	*customers, local events, staffing*

Exercise 23 – Looking back, looking out

The purpose of this exercise is to train your team to think deeply about the organization's past experiences of its relationship with the outside world, and the influence this relationship has had on the business. Strategists tend not to do this particularly well, putting their efforts into futuristic thinking. Yet the stories in these past experiences carry secrets of future success.

This is an exercise that your team can do in their own time and then discuss their results in the learning group at the next meeting. It can be achieved in a number of ways, for example each person doing all the exercise, or the team collectively doing the first part of the exercise and pairs or individuals each taking one or two 'chapters'.

Show your team the example of the restaurant above, then set up the following exercise.

1. List *all* the relationships that your organization or your department has with the outside world, that is – obvious contacts as well as less obvious influences. In the view that every relationship has a story to tell, imagine you are to write a book about these relationships. Put together a synopsis for this book in the following way.
2. Build your book on the basis of a different chapter for each relationship. Give each chapter a *title* and in some way convey the *theme* of that relationship, that is, the story in the relationship and how the relationship has impacted on the business. There may even be different sections in each

chapter, as in my example below on staffing. You can describe your theme through words (quotes, statements, prose, poetry, rhyme, song) or pictures (photographs, posters, magazine cuttings, illustrations, cartoons, patterns). I would recommend you use a variety of different ways in your synopsis, as that will help stretch your thinking process.

Have fun.

For example

Title:	Apple turnover
Theme:	The tension between familiarity and efficiency
The story:	Many of the staff are from the local community who are well known. Lack of availability of trained staff locally has led to a *laissez-faire* approach to their work from the kitchen staff and waitresses.

SUMMARY

Knowledge and experiences from the past inform our thinking in many ways, but even then there are times when we miss the obvious. Finding ways of stimulating our thinking process to take in a much wider range of information is the task you have to face; train the mind to think differently. Looking back also means 'seeing' the past in a number of different ways, allowing different perspectives to clearly see the mountains, rivers and plains of reality from different aspects, rather than a mere landscape painting hanging on the wall.

Looking back also means 'seeing' the past in a number of different ways

CHAPTER 8

WHAT'S HAPPENING NOW?

KEY LEARNING POINTS

■ Understand the components of a S.W.O.T. analysis
■ Be able to do a S.W.O.T. analysis

The present is something that moves; it is not permanent or fixed. What is today may be different tomorrow, next week, next month, in six months' time. This is important because it means that strategic thinking must be a dynamic process. One of the skills of a successful strategist is to remain responsive to changes in the environment which might contrast the stability of the organization.

Remember the saying '[chance] opportunity favours the prepared mind'. Being prepared means on the one hand holding the sense of purpose, and on the other looking out to observe movement in the environment, responding to that movement when it offers up new opportunities or the best opportunities. We see this process in nature, for example in spring birds time their nesting in relation to changing weather conditions. The idea is that offspring hatch at a time when there is an abundance of food. Weather conditions can delay or precipitate spring growth. Birds respond to this to ensure that their offspring have the best chance of survival. In Darwinian terms, the purpose of 'survival of the species' is held constant while the species makes the best of opportunities in the environment for achieving this.

S.W.O.T. ANALYSIS

One way that conventional strategist assess the current situation for a business is through a S.W.O.T. analysis. This is a prescriptive approach, holding an assumption that organizations are successful when they intentionally adapt to their environment. The S.W.O.T analysis is a strategic tool to identify consistency between the capability of an organization and the demands of the environment – internal and external. This analysis is then used to guide actions that build on the organization's strengths, overcome weaknesses, secure opportunities consistent with strengths, and avoid threats. There are six environments that a business, commercial or public sector, needs to consider in a S.W.O.T. analysis (Garrett 1995). These are:

> S.W.O.T. analysis is a prescriptive approach, holding an assumption that organizations are successful when they intentionally adapt to their environment

- Political
- Physical
- Economic
- Social
- Technological
- Trade.

Keeping these six environments in mind, the analysis goes like this:

- *Strengths* are areas of value within the organization.
- *Weaknesses* are the liabilities within the organization.
- *Opportunities* are favourable or advantageous combinations of circumstances that provide the organization with opportunities to explore new directions.
- *Threats* are possible risks that could threaten the viability and future success of the organization.

Remember, strengths and weaknesses are internal to the organization, whereas opportunities and threats are external to the organization.

STRENGTHS

Strengths can be tangible or intangible, personal or impersonal.

For example

- Having a highly respected charismatic leader.
- Having a world-recognized 'guru' as a key figure in the organization, for instance in educational and research institutions.
- Producing a leading edge product before your competitors for which there is already a demand – often seen in the world of IT.

WEAKNESSES

Often an organization decides to invest in developing new business strategies because it has recognized organizational weaknesses. There might also be threats of weakening in the future.

For example, some typical weaknesses include:

- Trends towards late deliveries, diminishing customer service.
- Increasing staff turnover, especially skilled staff.
- Products or services becoming outdated or obsolete. For example, in the field of management consultancy throughout the 1970s and 1980s outdoor team building was seen by many as 'the best thing since sliced bread'; in the 1990s organizations are looking for team

> development that offers more integrated learning that
> will impact on the business in a different way – that
> will give the business 'added value'.

As you work with your team you could ask them to come up
with some more examples, especially related to your industry
and organization.

OPPORTUNITIES

Identifying existing or potential opportunities for the business
to grow is constant for the strategist. Your team can probably
come up with their own ideas but the sort of situation that
might arise is:

- The announcement of government grant-aid for special
  community projects.
- An improving business climate.
- A competitor that is experiencing quality control
  problems, late products or low quality service delivery,
  etc.
- A new retail development going up on the outskirts of a
  nearby town.

THREATS

Threats are the reverse of opportunities. They are situations
that could threaten the viability of future success of the
organization, for example:

- Increased competition.
- Competitors recently reducing their prices – this is typical
  in the fuels industry where regular changes take place
  between competitors.
- A new retail development going up on the outskirts of a
  nearby town (this could be an opportunity for one
  business or a threat to another).

You can work through the S.W.O.T. analysis in Exercise 24
with your team, but before you do that let's just look at the

restaurant as an example and how the analysis changes with the death of Caroline's father.

On the basis of what we know so far, if we had done a S.W.O.T. analysis on the restaurant before Caroline's father died it would probably have looked something like the following example:

Example – S.W.O.T. analysis before the proprietor's death

Internal	External
Strengths	**Opportunities**
The owner's charismatic style with customers	Building on the river setting
Mutual respect between owner and staff	Ambience of the buildings
Well-established business	
Many regular customers	
Beautiful environment over-looking the river	
Can offer winter and summer environments	
Spacious	
Weaknesses	**Threats**
Variety of food is not high priority	Increasing local competition
Standard of food preparation could be questionable	Changing customer needs in their eating habits
Inward rather than outward looking	

Example – S.W.O.T. analysis immediately after *the proprietor's death*

Internal	External
Strengths	**Opportunities**
Enthusiasm of Caroline and Mark to keep the business going *Beautiful environment overlooking the river* *Can offer winter and summer environments* *Spacious*	Recognizing that there is a wide interest locally in vegetarian food Otherwise unknown
Weaknesses	**Threats**
No charismatic figure to carry the business Relationship between family and staff under question No experience by Caroline or Mark in running a business *Variety of food is not high priority* *Standard of food preparation could be questionable* *Inward rather than outward looking*	New competition coming into the area Otherwise unknown

The main point of this example is that within a very short space of time the attributes of an analysis can change. What may be a strength today, could be a weakness tomorrow. What may be a weakness in one context could be a strength in another. The strategic thinker needs to remain flexible and fluid, not rigid and fixed.

What may be a strength today, could be a weakness tomorrow

STRATEGIC ALIGNMENT

There is a further important aspect of the opportunities and threats in a S.W.O.T analysis that will add value to your thinking. When exploring opportunities and threats it can help if you take into consideration more generic strategies that the organization is pursuing. This aspect of strategic thinking was developed by Michael Porter of the Harvard Business School in the 1980s. In principle this approach looks at:

- How commercial organizations establish the basis on which they build and sustain competitive advantage.
- How public service organizations can provide value for money – in other words, how they can sustain the quality of service within agreed budgets.

The focus is on three fundamental principles:

1. *Cost leadership* – Where a business aims for low-cost leadership, that is, having the lowest cost compared to competitors over a given period of time.
2. *Differentiation* – Where a business seeks to be unique in its industry.
3. *Focus* – Where a business 'narrows down' its competitive scope within a target segment. It tailors its strategy to serve within a target market to the exclusion of other markets. This can be either cost or differentiation focused.

Many companies become stuck because they are not clear what their generic strategy is. Porter's approach encourages the strategic thinker to consider more deeply and then to clarify the competitive advantage the business seeks to achieve.

Exercise 24 – S.W.O.T. analysis

1. To build your team's thinking in this arena, first invite them to brainstorm a *general* or typical range of strengths, weaknesses, opportunities and threats without focusing as yet on your own organization. You could have a flip chart for each one. Your role will be to make sure they keep internal and external suggestions in the appropriate places. Apart from that allow the freedom of the brainstorm to occur without judgement.
2. Next, discuss with your team, if you and your team were

setting up your own restaurant what competitive advantage would you aim for and why?

3. Whether you are a commercial organization or public sector organization, what is the angle that your organization has taken to achieve and sustain a 'competitive advantage'? If a clear angle has not been taken, what would the team recommend and how could it achieve its recommendations?

4. Once your team are in the spirit of the exercise, get them to do a S.W.O.T. analysis on your organization's current status using the chart below. You could assign the different categories to small groups or pairs. Consider:
   - What are the strengths?
   - What are the weaknesses?
   - What opportunities now exist (or are likely to exist soon) that the business could be taking advantage of?
   - What are some current (or looming) threats to the continuing success of the business?

Internal	External
Strengths	**Opportunities**
Weaknesses	**Threats**

The S.W.O.T. analysis has been criticized for its simplicity and the view that the right strategy can be selected before action is taken. Yet frequently neglected are blocks that the organization's culture and power structure can impose on the implementation of a strategy.

Culture is the collective behaviour of the people within the organization. The strategist must be aware of the collective behaviours that could undermine a strategy. Chapter 7 discussed some of these in the stories and rituals that exist within an organization.

Power structures are the structures of authority and status within a political system. The strategist needs to be aware of two dimensions of power:

1. Where strategy implementation may become blocked, and how.
2. Who is influential and who they need to influence. The saying that goes with this is 'it's not what you know, it's who you know' – but, of course, it's both.

The naive strategists will lose their potency if they ignore these two important aspects of the business.

The wise strategists can make sure provision is built in to overcome cultural and power obstacles in advance of action.

SUMMARY

At the start of this chapter I mentioned the dynamic process of the present and then pursued the S.W.O.T. analysis as a tool for assessing the current state of the business. The value of a S.W.O.T. analysis lies in getting the strategic thinker to consider certain important areas in relation to the business; it helps their thinking. However, analyses have their limitations, for instance they are a snapshot of a moment in time. Where complex analyses are necessary, by the time the results appear they are already history, especially in the rapidly changing world that we live in today. If strategists rely only on the outcome of their analysis to inform their thinking they will be constrained by this. They need to think beyond these limits to stay informed. Chapter 9 will go on to explore key factors that the strategic thinker can also take into account.

CHAPTER 9

*K*EY FACTORS

KEY LEARNING POINTS

■ Understand the concept of critical success factors
■ Know how to identify critical success factors
■ Be able to set some measurable outcomes against which critical success factors can be assessed
■ Be able to identify key assumptions
■ Be able to challenge limiting factors when they are presented

In this chapter there are three areas that you and your team will learn about that will influence your thinking:

1. *Critical success factors*   Factors that are critical to the success of the organization.
2. *Key assumptions*   Underlying assumptions upon which the organization will base its plan to implement its strategy. These assumptions can be either explicit and clearly defined, or implicit within the functioning of the organization.
3. *Limiting factors*   Imposed limitations which people introduce that can reduce the potential of the organization. You will learn how to challenge limiting behaviour.

All three areas have an impact on strategic development.

CRITICAL SUCCESS FACTORS

Critical success factors are the few high priority areas which must go just right for the organization to succeed and flourish, with emphasis on *critical* and *few*. The organization must manage these factors well to be successful. In identifying critical success factors, more is not better; quality not quantity is the essence.

Associated with this are high priority areas which are the characteristics, conditions and variables that, when properly maintained and managed, can most positively impact the success of an organization.

Obviously the vision, developed in Chapter 10, and mission, developed in Chapter 11, will dictate which few factors will be critical in a given instance. But beware, critical success factors are only temporary. The following is a list of typical critical success factors for non-profit making organizations.

Example of some critical success factors in a non-profit making organization

- Funding
- Concurrence with laws
- Accountability
- Service orientation
- Public relations
- Trained staff
- Productivity

Critical success factors are not just for business

Critical success factors are not just for business. Just as strategic thinking can permeate many aspects of our life, so it is that we can personally pay attention to critical success factors as well. My son is currently taking his GCSEs. In watching his revision process I notice that he too has critical success factors that he attends to, but he doesn't call them critical success factors. His main concern is to achieve the highest possible grades in the subjects that he is taking. He has finished his main study and is into revision. The important factors for him now are:

- Revising each subject thoroughly
- Useful revision methods
- Past exam papers for each subject
- Understanding exam processes
- Being well equipped with pens, pencils, etc. for each exam
- Stress reduction methods
- Getting a good night's sleep before each exam
- And a factor that I have introduced, 'to cut down on his social life until after his exams'!

Scenario – The paratrooper

A paratrooper team are preparing for a parachute jump. It is their first. Their main concern is to survive the jump and there are a number of critical success factors that they need to consider in their *preparation* for the jump:

- Pilot skill
- Their training
- Equipment availability and condition
- Altitude
- Luck

Understanding the critical success factors beforehand will help the paratroopers put extra time into the areas that matter and preparation for the jump.

OUTCOMES

With critical success factors come identifiable 'outcomes', which are observable or measurable results of the actions you take. They are evidence that critical success factors are being achieved. For example, a measurable outcome for a public broadcasting station with a critical success factor of 'adequate funding' might be annual contributions (increase or decrease) over the next three years. This procedure is important in strategic planning activities because it ensures that the team become involved in meaningful activities, not 'busy work'.

Exercise 25 – Critical success factors

The purpose of these exercises is to help your team understand and identify for themselves *critical success factors* and measurable *outcomes*. You can choose to run one, two, or all three exercises.

1. Get the team to consider what would be the critical success factors for the actual parachute jump in the paratrooper scenario.
2. Earlier in this chapter we identified some critical success factors for non-profit making organizations. Now get your team to come up with some examples for profit making organizations.
3. The next task requires your team to turn again to the restaurant scenario. You can adapt the exercise by adjusting the time limits.

    Caroline and Mark have developed a draft mission – 'Being renowned for a healthy eating approach in their menus'. You are to set up a role play in which the local newspaper interviews Caroline and Mark and some of their customers, *five years in the future*. Two people play the roles of Caroline and Mark. Two people act as interviewers for the local paper who are running a special article on successful businesses. The rest of the team are clients of the restaurant.

The interviewers (10 minutes)
The key to the interview is:

■ To come up with *five* critical success factors which Caroline and Mark would have needed to pay attention to.
■ The rationale behind these factors.
■ The measurable outcomes.

Explore how you might acquire the information you need from the clientele and proprietors of the restaurant. Come up with at least five questions that will help you to get this information and discover important factors that were missed.

Caroline and Mark (10 minutes)
Allow yourselves to get into role and to feel a real sense of the mission, that is, a 'healthy eating' approach to menus, and how it has been achieved. Consider what your strategy was, how you set about achieving your mission five years ago and events that have occurred since which have forced you to change direction. In other words, create your scenario.

You may wish to visit the client group for up to 3 minutes during this session to gain their opinion of the service you have provided.

Clientele (10 minutes)

You were customers of the restaurant before Caroline's father died and have continued being so. The changes have been quite dramatic, especially with regard to the new 'healthy eating' menu.

Use your imagination to discuss the changes that have taken place and name five important factors that you believe have contributed to the success of the business. These may include a change in direction along the way. Caroline and Mark may wish to meet with you during this session for up to 3 minutes to gain your views on the service they have provided.

The Interview (10 minutes)

Set up the role play in which the interviewers achieve their objective and acquire enough information for their article.

Now step out of role.

Discuss as a team what you have learned from the exercise about critical success factors and measurable outcomes, in the context of strategic thinking.

KEY ASSUMPTIONS

These are important assumptions upon which the organization is basing its plans for implementing its strategy. In any planning activity the strategists must make certain assumptions about factors typically not under the organization's control.

Some they may document, others remain unspoken. For example:

- The organization's mission will remain unchanged for at least two years.
- The organization's operating budget will be reduced by 20 per cent per year for the next three years.
- The economy will grow at 10 per cent per year and inflation will not exceed 3 per cent per year.
- No major breakthroughs will occur within the next 10 years to make our product obsolete.

- It will be possible to identify and hire qualified computer scientists over the next six years.
- The bank will support the overdraft facility for at least two years.

You will not achieve the success you desire unless you also identify the critical assumptions you have made before moving on.

The key assumptions provide several aids to strategic planning, such as:

- They help you identify and quantify risk factors.
- They identify areas where the team may need to investigate further before committing to a strategy.

Exercise 26 – Identifying key assumptions

1. With your team take a few minutes to brainstorm some key assumptions that Caroline and Mark would have had to make in their five-year strategy. Do not pass judgement on people's ideas. Write these up on a flip chart.
2. Get your team to name some key assumptions that you believe your business and/or department needs to make in relation to its survival and success over the next five years.
3. As a third optional question, you could get your team to independently look at their career paths and identify the key assumptions that they have to make in relation to their career aspirations. Allow some time for team members to share these, either in pairs or all together as a team.

LIMITING FACTORS

Tell me what precisely are the limiting factors that have convinced you nothing can be done?

Ohmae (1982)

So far in this chapter we have looked at the positive side of strategic thinking. Frequently, however, people get caught up in a 'nothing can be done' syndrome, especially when the future looks grim, or there is a 'felt' loss of control. Constantly

Frequently people get caught up in a 'nothing can be done' syndrome

FIGURE 9.1 Overcoming limiting factors

identifying those things which cannot be done and looking for the possibilities that are left will leave the strategist in an impossible position.

One of the tasks of the strategist is to constantly ask challenging questions of themselves and people around them, such as those illustrated in Figure 9.1. One way of doing this is by taking a third party view; that is, stepping outside the situation and looking back into the situation, objectively.

The skill for the strategist lies in generating an awareness, that is, getting people to articulate what the ideal state might be, even if it does not seem possible to achieve just yet. You would be surprised at the powerfulness of this process in terms of unblocking the flow and releasing new energy.

Limiting factors can often be seen as limiting patterns of behaviour and limiting ways of thinking in a culture. The skill lies in not getting drawn in, but staying outside of this pattern and challenging it.

The skill lies in not getting drawn in, but staying outside of this pattern and challenging it

Exercise 27 – Challenging limiting behaviour

This exercise will take approximately 45 minutes and will train your team to challenge limiting behaviour rather than accept it as a constraint.

1. Get a pack of blank cards and give six to each member of your team.
2. Get them to title three of the cards with TEAM and the other three with ORGANIZATION.
3. On each of the three TEAM cards get them to draw a picture or in some way illustrate a limiting behaviour or pattern that exists in the team, for example team members are constantly in firefighting mode, or always find a reason why something won't work.
4. Next, on the other three cards get team members to name three different limiting behaviours that exist in the organization.
5. Collect up the cards in their separate piles of TEAM and ORGANIZATION. Shuffle both piles well. Deal three cards to each team member from each pack. Don't be concerned if it appears that there are repetitions in the packs – use them constructively.
6. On the cards that they receive get team members to think of a statement that someone would say that expresses the point illustrated or behaviour named, for example 'we never have time to think about changing the way that we work'. It might help to think of this in the context of a problem arising. Then write this on the other side of the card.
7. Finally, collect the cards again in two piles and shuffle them. Give three cards from each pile to each team member. This time their task is to come up with a challenging response from a third party position. So if they were outside the organization looking in, what would they say that would challenge the limitation.

Share your results in the team or small groups. If you are working with small groups get them to come up with the four most significant limitations, two *from each set of cards* and explain to the rest of the team how they would challenge each limitation.

SUMMARY

Along the path of success are signposts that inform you as to whether you are coming from, and going to, your desired direction. The signposts in determined strategy are the critical success factors. In determining your route you identify the critical success factors on your map. Yet before setting off on a journey there are many assumptions that you have to make, for example about the predictability of the weather, the changing path underfoot, the time it will take to cover certain distances, that the signposts have not been vandalized along the way. Awareness of these assumptions helps us plan and prepare.

Finally, there are factors in your self-limitations. What capacity do you have to make this journey? How will you cope with the unexpected? Do you have the stamina? What damage will you incur if you fail? Asking these questions when sat down at a table with a map in front of you can be self limiting. Developing skills to challenge this behaviour in yourself and in others is essential for the strategic thinker and your capacity to stretch beyond current boundaries into new unexplored territory.

CHAPTER 10

THE VISION

KEY LEARNING POINTS

This chapter will help you develop your team's skills in a visioning process, as well as explore some limiting factors that can diminish the potential of a vision. Your team will develop a vision through three different metaphorical characters – an explorer, an artisan and a judge – and experiment with language to increase the potency of the vision. This chapter will enable your team to:

■ Understand the principles of setting a vision
■ Be able to create a vision and articulate it for others to support
■ Understand personal blocks that could diminish the visioning process
■ Create a personal vision through a visioning process

VISION

Visioning could be defined as a mental picture of what the organization could look like, feel like, act like, sound like and be seen as in the future. Visioning is the process for assessing the future and speculating what may be. It is a popular strategists' tool and is by no means as simplistic as looking into a crystal ball.

... purpose without vision has no sense of appropriate scale.
Senge (1990)

To create a vision you need to change your frame of reference:

From	To
Today	The future
Looking backward from now	Looking forward from now
Current circumstances	Future successes
Current assumptions	Assumptions required to achieve future success

Visioning exercises are like firing an arrow into the future, defining an image of what future success is all about, as defined in Figure 10.1.

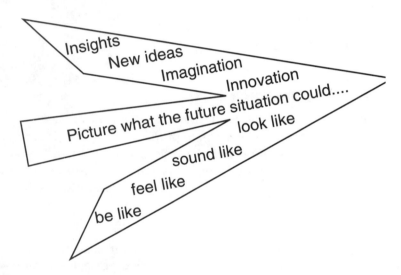

FIGURE 10.1 Visioning arrow

THE ATTRIBUTES OF VISION

Having a vision enables you and your team to see the direction in which the organization is heading. You align and plan your actions today towards achieving the successes of tomorrow. Determined strategy implies that greatness is achieved through having a vision. Creating a vision in determined strategy is different to a visioning process in emergent strategy, as you will discover in Part 3.

Here are six pointers that will help you and your team understand visioning in more depth. The vision is:

Purpose is discussed in detail in Chapter 3

1. *Powerful* The power of the vision lies in the tension that is created between what could be in the future and what is happening now.
2. *Purposeful* Vision cannot be understood in isolation; in particular it needs to be linked to purpose and core values.
3. *Self-determining* Vision is not relative. If vision is linked to competition then it might be that the vision stops short of achieving greatness because that is what the competition has done.
4. *Concrete* Where purpose is abstract and instils a sense of direction, vision is concrete – a specific destination, an image of a desired future.
5. *Multi-faceted* Vision is multi-faceted, for example including:
   - Material facets such as wealth
   - Personal facets such as health, integrity
   - Altruistic facets such as helping in the community.
6. *Emotional* Visions are intrinsically linked to emotions that become the driving force towards achieving the vision.

Visioning is not an easy way of thinking for most of us; we tend to focus on today's problems, realities and constraints and to base our day to day decisions on past experiences rather than future expectations. Establishing a vision means asking such questions as 'What could we become?' or 'Where would I like to be in five years' time?' or 'Where is the industry going and where would we like our business to be in relation to the industry?'

In many organizations the vision is determined by the *few* and followed by the *many*. Followers need to be responsive to and supportive of the new ideas if innovative leadership is to be legitimized and the business is to succeed. Yet it would be foolish if people believed that visioning is only for those at the top. On the contrary, we all have the capacity to create visions and work towards them, whether they are organizational visions, departmental visions, team visions or personal visions. Either way, the vision will need to fit in with a wider pattern of things if it is to be a success.

Visioning means anticipating the future, being creative

and exploratory, willing to take risks and remaining open to learning. Peter Senge (1990) in his book *The Fifth Discipline* explains how vision creates a tension like an elastic band between the future and current reality. In the view that tension seeks release there are only two ways that the situation can be resolved, either by pulling reality toward the vision or pulling the vision toward reality. The skill lies in holding a steady vision.

> ... how bold is your vision? Bold enough for you to be comfortable?
> Sworder (1995)

CREATING A TEAM VISION

You can use three different role characters to inform you in the visioning process:

- The explorer
- The artisan
- The judge.

These characters are within us all, to a greater or lesser extent.

THE EXPLORER

Creative thinking is not devoid of facts, concepts or experiences. Like an explorer it is necessary for strategists to put forth the effort to look at new things, gain new experiences and also look at old things in new ways. During the course of searching explorers look for unusual patterns, unanticipated relationships and contrary-to-logic notions.

THE ARTISAN

Having pulled together a new framework of ideas, you have to shift gear and release the artisan within yourself. Like an artist you need to look for patterns. In Chapter 4 there is an exercise which talks about 'What if . . .?' questions (Exercise 7). Well, the artisan will use this process to look for hidden similarities and analogies among seemingly different concepts and clusters of facts. Having done so, you are likely to come up with a new idea or two. You do not care, as an artisan, whether your new ideas seem to others harebrained or practical. At this stage it doesn't matter.

THE JUDGE

As a judge you critically evaluate your new ideas. You ask
yourself questions such as:

- Does this idea have merit?
- If it could be achieved, would the results be worthwhile
  for the organization?
- Could we sell this idea to stakeholders?
- Are there any drawbacks?
- Is the timing right?

Ultimately, you make a decision, even if it is a gut decision.

You and your team can borrow from each of the
techniques that the different roles present. You will probably
have a combination of different strengths you can draw on for
harnessing a vision. Although we all have the capacity to
engage with all three characters within ourselves, many of us
have one in which we are more talented. It is the combination
of your team's talents that will help you create a vision.

Exercise 28 – Creating a team vision

For this exercise you will need a flip chart, some A5 card in two
different colours, thick felt tip pens and a pack of sticky dots.

In this exercise you will get your team to create a vision for
the restaurant using the three characters above. You will do this
by 'stepping into the shoes or boots' of each character as they
appear in the visioning process.

Imagine your team have been asked by Caroline and Mark
to create a vision for the future of their restaurant. Work together
through the following steps.

Step 1 – Step into the boots of the explorer

Using a form similar to the one shown below, pull together some
facts and information which you already have on the restaurant.
Clarify the assumptions that you make about the current running
of the business.

Historical facts
(Example) *It is well established in the community*

Key Information
(Example) *There are other explorers out there fighting for business*

Assumptions
(Example) *People are interested in variety and specialities on the menu*

Next, brainstorm ideas that could lead to a vision for the future of the restaurant. Draw on the talents of your explorer. Release the constraints of your mind, allowing your adventurous selves to emerge.

Capture each one of these ideas on a different card, each card containing a different idea, for example vegetarian menus, a restaurant called 'Connections' where tables are linked through a telephone system and the theme is 'make friends with a stranger', etc.

Once you have a range of ideas, move onto the next step.

Step 2 – Step into the shoes of the artisan

Get a sense of the artisan within yourself and what that means to you. Here your task is to develop the explorer ideas of the restaurant further by engaging in 'What if ...?' questions, by bringing together ideas and forming patterns, coming up with harebrained artistic ideas and allowing visions to emerge.

You can develop the 'What if...?' exercise by introducing pairs of opposites; for example 'What if I ...?

- Expand/reduce
- Keep going/give in
- Capture it/free it
- Change it/leave it as it is
- Take on more staff/reduce number of staff.

Use the cards from Step 1 in a way that enhances your artistic process. The idea is to move the ideas from the explorer to forming tangible visions. On a different set of coloured card capture your developing visions.

Step 3 – Step into the shoes of the judge
Get in touch with your judge and formulate a set of questions that you need to ask.

With the new set of vision cards from Step 2, critically evaluate each vision one at a time. Go through your questions, and refer to the questions identified earlier in this chapter under 'The judge'.

If you need to develop a vision further, write the new vision on a different card of the same colour, discarding the old one.

It is now decision-making time. When you have exhausted the questioning process lay the cards out in front of you. Give each member of your team three sticky dots. They should then place their dots on the cards that carry the vision/s of their choice. They can use their dots in any way they wish, that is, they could put all three dots on the same card.

Out of this you will probably have one or two visions for the restaurant that most people subscribe to.

Your next step will be to put the vision into a meaningful language that others can relate to.

ARTICULATING THE VISION
Having created your vision you need to articulate it to the people who need to subscribe to it and who will be working towards achieving it. You may want to take time to increase the power of the vision through your use of language. Use of metaphors and analogies can create fresh meaning in a vision.

Visions need to:

- Be inspiring

- Be clear, sharp and concise
- Be unambiguous
- Be flexible
- Show how value can be added to the business.

Exercise 29 – Putting the vision into words

This exercise should take approximately 20 minutes.

Using the preferred vision for the restaurant from the last exercise, get your team to work in small groups for approximately 15 minutes and experiment with the language of the vision using the key points identified above. One way of experimenting with language is to make good use of a thesaurus and dictionary.

By the end of this exercise your team should have come up with a clear workable vision.

You could, of course, go through the last two exercises to formulate your team's vision in their real work, or a vision for your organization.

FANCIFUL OR POSSIBLE?

Different people create different sorts of visions. For example, optimists may overestimate what can be achieved, while pessimists may underestimate the possibilities. You may have noticed a variation in your team in the last two exercises. When working with a team it is important to build on different views to find a vision to which everyone can subscribe.

Visioning is a way of stretching the boundaries of what people believe they can achieve, like stretching an elastic band – enough stretch to feel challenged but not too much that you give up.

People often have difficulty with the gap between the vision and their current reality. The gaps can make the vision seem unrealistic, leaving people feeling hopeless. For example 'I would like to renovate a barn to live in', but 'I don't have the capital'. The 'buts' can make a vision seem impossible to achieve, yet it is the creative energy in the tension that makes the impossible become possible. With the vision in place you

... genuine caring about a shared vision is rooted in personal visions. Senge (1990)

begin a creative process that will enable the impossible to become possible, for example 'I will creatively seek to finance my vision'. You set goals, make plans and give yourself timescales.

Many people believe that once a vision is in place things come your way that help you achieve your vision. Alternatively, it might be that you respond to opportunities that you otherwise might not have noticed.

Having a vision enables what seems impossible to become possible.

PERSONAL LIMITATIONS

As children we start life with tremendous creativity, developing a sense of power as we grow. However, our powerfulness is frequently chipped away by comments and behaviours from adults who tell us or infer that we '*can't* have' or '*don't* do' certain things. Repeatedly undermining a child's sense of power can leave them feeling powerless.

Concern for children's well-being can also lead to overprotecting them and denying them the opportunity to take risks. It is through taking risks that children learn about their limitations and their potential.

Many children are repeatedly told that they are not good enough or hopeless at tasks. This message comes from parents, teachers, peers and the social system. For example, our system of secondary and grammar education in the 1960s and 1970s implied 'not good enough' to pupils who went to secondary schools.

Low self-worth can deplete the quality of strategic thinking and visioning processes

Equally our lack of self-worth can contribute to lack of vision. Repeated comments as children that we are 'not good enough' or that we are 'hopeless at' can have a profound effect on our capabilities as adults resulting in 'fear of failure' or even 'fear of success'. Also, it isn't necessarily what people say, it can be implied by parents, teachers, peers and the social system.

Deep inner beliefs about ourselves do not change at the flick of a switch. They take time to change. Change requires willingness to learn and constant exposure to new and challenging experiences.

We need to create environments in which we support people in their learning and risk taking. When mistakes are made we should encourage learning through feedback that is supportive, rather than through reprimand that is unsupportive. Much of our work in organizations today lies in tapping into the potential which people possess that has been undermined in the past; potential that has, for many, never been realized. As individuals our task is also to discover our own personal power and self-worth, regaining lost confidence to be creative and to take risks.

Scenario – Personal vision

At 33 years old and a mother of two young children, I had a vision of gaining a degree in psychology. The subject had always fascinated me but I had never had the opportunity to learn more about it. I left school before taking GCEs, believing that I was not good enough and scared that I would fail. It now meant taking GCSEs and 'A' levels before I did anything else, and for many reasons, especially financial, it seemed that my only route beyond that was through the Open University. I had my vision and started working towards it. Within a few months all sorts of things had come my way that ultimately made it possible for me to attend a university as a full-time mature student. My hours fitted perfectly with both caring for my children and studying. Money was not plentiful but we survived. Not only did I gain my degree but I also gained the experience of mingling with other students. I loved it. I believed that I could make it happen, and ultimately I realized my vision.

Working towards achieving a vision means not giving up what in your heart you believe to be possible.

Inner beliefs which influence or negate the development and perseverance for achieving personal vision will influence or impede visioning processes at work, in your own achievements and in your teams, in the department and the organization.

Deep inner beliefs about yourself don't change at the flick of a switch. They change through your willingness to learn, through constant exposure to new and challenging experiences which dis-confirm negative beliefs and help you realize your potential. You cannot do this alone. You need other people around you to point out when you are achieving and when you have acted powerfully. Simply because it is not within your frame of thinking to start with, you are not always conscious of your own potential. Above all, creating an environment that supports learning allows people to take risks and encourages constructive feedback processes.

Exercise 30 – Personal visioning

Many executives, managers, academics and professionals are realizing the power of visualization. Here is an exercise that you could do with your team either as a group exercise following the format below, or by giving each person the visualization to read and work through in their own time. The exercise is about creating a personal vision.

Check that your team are sitting comfortably and that there are not too many disturbances around you. Some people visualize better if they close their eyes – you might like to suggest this to your team as an option. Then talk them slowly through 'The dream' below. When I do this with groups and teams I often find that I need to talk more slowly than feels comfortable to me to allow people to fully construct their images.

The dream

Imagine that tomorrow you discovered you could do something that you always dreamed of but never thought possible. Notice how you feel about this and what you believe it would take to fulfil your dream.

Take yourself forward to five years' time, having followed your dream. Notice how far along your dream path you are; what

you have achieved so far, what you have discovered in yourself that has enabled you to follow your dream in this way.
Notice your achievements.
Notice where you are and what you are doing.
Notice the environment around you.
Notice what the weather is like, what time of year it is.
What are the colours and smells around you?
Get a sense of people, who they are, how you relate to them and they to you.
Notice what it has taken for you to follow your dream.
Imagine you are in reflective mood, looking back over these five years. You have been asked by a close friend to name three insights or three things that you discovered about yourself and your potential that enabled you to reach this stage in your dream fulfilment.
Now bring yourself back to today.

When your team are ready, encourage some sharing of visions, without any pressure to 'reveal all'. Some people may not wish to share their vision.

You could also do this part of the exercise in pairs.

SUMMARY

A vision is merely giving light to direction. The direction is purpose. New visions emerge as old ones are achieved; the purpose lives on.

Creating a vision can be powerful, especially when personal limitations and inhibitions are removed. Holding a vision frames the mind to be open to opportunities which might otherwise be missed. A vision will make possible what otherwise might not even be considered. In organizations the essence lies in involving others such that they own the vision and take it into their work.

There are many techniques that can be used to establish a vision. Two different examples have been used here, one in developing a team vision, the other in establishing personal vision. There is increased energy and motivation to move towards the vision when personal vision and organizational visions are aligned. The techniques described here can be adapted to suit many different situations.

CHAPTER 11

THE MISSION

KEY LEARNING POINTS

- Understand the purpose of a mission
- Be able to integrate the components of a mission into a cohesive whole
- Know how to create a mission statement that employees can work with

This chapter will show you how to develop your team's skills in pulling together the necessary components for a mission. Not all organizations work with a mission, so it is not essential that you have one. However, as you learn how to develop a mission you will get a feel of the depth of meaning behind the statement and the added value that a mission statement could bring to your work. You can then judge the worth of a mission statement for yourself.

Exercise 31 – Collecting together mission statements

A week before you introduce this chapter to your team, get them to seek out at least three different mission statements each from different companies that they know of, or are connected with in their work or through books and the media. Encourage them to bring a variety of statements, especially differentiating between profit making and non-profit making organizations. You will use these in a later exercise.

It will be useful for you to do this exercise as well, seeking out some particularly good mission statements in your industry. Ideally you will have 10 or more in each grouping.

THE PURPOSE OF A MISSION

- A mission is a nebulous concept, hard to define and hard to pin down. It has no beginning and no end, it just *is*.
- An organizations's mission is a particular path that an organization decides to take; a path that is anticipated will add value to the business.
- A statement of the mission will encapsulate in a cohesive whole the purpose, vision and strategy for achieving that vision.
- A mission statement is not a vision of the future, although it carries the vision within it.
- A mission statement will guide management and staff in their work, *in the present*.
- A mission can provide the glue for bringing people together in working towards a common goal. Because the mission is a vessel which carries the vision, purpose, values and strategy of the business, it is the guiding principle for decisions and actions of management and staff. It can help people understand the reason for doing the things that they do and the way that they do them.

Communicating a mission is not about putting a statement in pretty colours on the wall of the foyer or the office, but rather drawing in your team and staff to take onboard the mission as an all-embracing concept that they can work with. An organization's mission has to be integrated into the system; the heart, mind, body and spirit of the whole organization, starting from the top. It should not just be pinned to the wall in some vain hope that something worthwhile will seep into the woodwork.

Teams can establish a mission of their own, but these need to be aligned to the organization's mission.

DEVELOPING A MISSION

To develop a mission you need to ask five questions which you have already learned about in previous chapters. Each question carries a basic principle that is important to developing a mission. (These have also been discussed in previous chapters, as shown in brackets.)

The question	The principle
1. Why does the company exist?	*Purpose* (Chapter 3)
2. What does the company believe in?	*Core values* (Chapter 5)
3. What is distinctive about the company?	*Strengths* (Chapter 8)
4. What could the company become?	*Vision* (Chapter 10)
5. What are the behaviour standards that the company subscribes to?	*Behaviour guidelines which underpin the value system* (Chapter 3)

The best way to understand these questions is to work with them.

Exercise 32 – Developing a mission

Split your team into pairs or small groups, with each group or pair taking one *Principle* from the list above. Get your team to reflect on their learning and develop the components of a mission through the following exercise. The team may need to refer back to earlier learning in the named chapters.

For this exercise allow 15–20 minutes to address the questions below, then about five minutes for each group or pair to present to the whole team a brief overview of their findings and their answer to *The question*.

1. Describe the *Principle*, for example what is meant by *purpose*.
2. Could an organization be successful without this concept in the mission?

3. Then answer *The question* connected to the *Principle* in relation to the restaurant that Caroline and Mark are running in the scenario, for example, why does the company (business) exist?

Allow time between each presentation for a brief discussion and to challenge your team where there appear to be disagreements.

Keep all this information. It will be developed further in Exercise 34.

Alternative exercises

- Get your team to answer *The question* connected to the *Principle* in relation to your organization.
- Split your team into two groups and get both groups to address all five components. Present back to each other valuing the differences that arise out of the exercise. These differences will add weight to the thinking of the group. Develop each component until you have group consensus.
- This exercise could be applied equally well to establish a team's mission, replacing the word *company* for *team* in the questions. It is significant here that you achieve team consensus on each component.

If a top team were developing a mission for the business they would need one or two days to work in depth through the five questions and principles.

The next step is to bring these five components together in a mission statement.

THE MISSION STATEMENT

The mission statement puts the organization's mission into words that people can relate to and use in their work. This means Keep It Simple (KIS).

Example of a non-profit making organization

'... humanitarian organization, led by volunteers, that provides relief to victims of disasters and helps people prevent, prepare for, and respond to emergencies.'
American Red Cross

Example of a profit making organization

'Be the company that everyone wants to work for; everyone wants to do business with; everyone wants to own.' Australian iron ore producer

Exercise 33 – Drafting a mission statement (KIS)

The purpose of this exercise is for your team to understand the importance of keeping mission statements simple, and how employees need to be able to connect the mission statement with their work.

You will need coloured card cut into shapes about the same size as an A5 sheet of paper, some ReMount adhesive or Blu-tak and some thick felt tip pens.

You will need at least 10 mission statements for each group (profit making and non-profit making organizations).

Head up two flip chart sheets or large pieces of brown paper, one for 'Profit making organizations' and one for 'Non-profit making organizations'. Then write the above statements on cards and stick on the appropriate chart. Invite your team to add their collection of mission statements to the flip charts in the same way.

In two groups, each group working with a different collection of mission statements (profit making or non-profit making organizations), get your team to group the cards according to KIS. One way of doing this is to imagine they are an employee of an organization and are given the statement as the company's mission. How easy would they find it to relate to and build their work around. Three groupings would be:

■ Easy to relate to
■ Moderately easy to relate to
■ Very difficult to understand.

You may prefer other types of grouping or to let your team to come up with their own. Groups should share their findings with each other, clarifying key issues that may have been raised in the exercise.

If you haven't been able to collect together enough mission statements within the team you could duplicate the statements that you have, mixing statements related to both profit making and non-profit making organizations, each group working with the same set of statements. Or get your team to all work together as one group.

Once your team have a clear sense of what a good mission statement is, move them on to the next exercise.

Exercise 34 – Drafting a mission statement

This exercise should take approximately 30 minutes. Here you will be able to develop the outcome from the mission in Exercise 32 into a draft mission statement. Whether you worked with the restaurant scenario, your own organization or your team, this exercise will adapt according to how you would like to progress.

Split your team into small groups and then ask them to do the following exercise. Make sure that they all work with the same mission – restaurant, organization or team.

By using the information that you gathered in Exercise 32 and building on your knowledge of KIS mission statements given in Exercise 33, draft five different possible mission statements that you think best capture the mission you are working with. Use language that is:

- Clear
- Active rather than passive
- Challenging
- Here-and-now oriented (that is, use 'be' rather than 'become').

Write these up on a flip chart. Through discussion add and eliminate words, discard the statements that least fit the mission, experiment until your group have arrived at a suitable draft mission statement.

When all groups have finished, share the draft statements that are left and repeat the elimination process.

You should now have a draft mission statement that the whole team is reasonably happy with, even though you might not have full consensus.

If this is an organizational or team mission statement you would then allow 'simmer' time over a few days, for reflection and checking with staff to see if this is a mission statement that can be worked with, one that evokes challenge and inspiration.

Missions emerge from the way people work together and those that are imposed from the top rarely take root. Stacey (1993)

SUMMARY

The mission must have energy that brings life into the working practices of employees, and carry an expectation of success for the organization. A strong sense of mission is felt when the five elements – purpose, vision, strategy, values and behaviour – are closely woven together. A sense of mission is important; it generates trust and a belief in the activities of the organization. It is a motivator and adds a rich essence which carries the five elements into people's work. Above all, a sense of mission provides the basis for making decisions and judgements.

One final thought – due to an ever-changing environment, strategies and values embedded in the mission could become inappropriate over time. Reinforcing them could block the way to success rather than enhance it. Like all working practices, the mission must have regular review and adjustment.

CHAPTER 12

BEYOND THE LIMITS

For managers to 'let go', to change attitudes and habits, and to develop their strategic thinking abilities, fundamental changes to their habitual thinking need to occur first if they are to contribute to the success of the enterprise.

Sworder (1995)

KEY LEARNING POINTS

- Be able to challenge your own and other people's thinking
- Be able to challenge your own and other people's behaviour
- Be able to challenge management perspectives

All the chapters so far have engaged with both the theory and practice of developing strategy. This chapter is dedicated purely towards hands-on skills development in strategic thinking. The reason for this is that strategic thinking is a discipline and like any discipline needs rigorous practice to perform well. That doesn't mean to say it can't be fun. In this chapter you have a variety of activities rather than exercises that you and your team can undertake in your work. The activities can be both fun and practical. These activities fall under three categories:

- Challenging thought processes
- Challenging behaviour
- Challenging management perspectives.

You can use these activities with your team at any time, in team meetings or as a daily discipline. Some activities may interest you, others may not. Take them one at a time or offer them up to your team to choose how they would like to practise them.

CHALLENGING THOUGHT PROCESSES

The strategic thinkers need sensitivity, insight and an inquisitive mind that can't help challenging the status quo
Ohmae (1982)

We have already touched on this area in Chapter 4. Here, you will take a more sophisticated look at some psychological blocks that undermine strategic thought processes, and ways of dealing with them.

SHOULDS

When I hear people say to me 'This is how it *should* be done', in most cases I feel constrained. What was a simple rule that helped learning has turned into a rigid and fixed process.

Creative insight is a smouldering ember that must be fanned constantly to glow. Ohmae (1982)

Throughout life we need the 'shoulds' in order to get a grip on how to do new things, and for our own personal safety. 'Shoulds' create the infrastructure by which we exist, and over time they can become habitual and brittle.

Let's take a look again at the restaurant before Caroline's father died.

Scenario – Shoulds in the restaurant

Caroline's father, Henry, had very rigid beliefs about how a restaurant should be run and what sort of food should be served. To start with, this worked really well. The staff were clear about cleanliness rules, the sort of food that they should and should not include on the menu, laying out of the restaurant tables and so on. Over the years they continued to operate these rules firmly; they would be passed on to new employees as they arrived. Henry was rigorous about cleanliness, what he thought people liked to eat and how the environment should be laid out.

Over time people lost sight of the purpose of the rules; they simply operated them like robots. Innovation was lost and staff always deferred to Henry when a problem arose.

When Henry died, the restaurant was thrown into chaos. The staff had had a very rigid set of rules to follow. They had lost their pillar for holding these rules up. When they thought about it they didn't even know *why* they were operating most of the rules. They could understand health and hygiene, but even then they recognized that there was more than one way of achieving this.

Rules are important – shoulds can be deadening. What can you do about it? There are at least two ways around this. In the first two activities you will find out.

ACTIVITY 1 – CHANGING A 'SHOULD'

This is very simple. Whenever you hear yourself or someone else using a should which seems based on a rigid viewpoint:

- See what happens if you change the word 'should' for 'could'. This immediately opens up the possibility of choice, without undermining important rules and guidelines.

ACTIVITY 2 – WHY SHOULD YOU?

This is more complex, but takes the problem to a deeper level of solution, to purpose:

■ Ask 'Why' five times.

For example

Caroline's father, Henry, always printed the menu in French as well as English.

1. *Why?*   He wanted to reflect the French cuisine.
2. *Why French cuisine?*   He wanted to be different from the other local restaurants.
3. *Why did he want to be different?*   Henry didn't want to be diverted by competition.
4. *Why avoid competition?*   It meant he had greater control of prices.
5. *Why have such control?*   It is easier to manage profit margins.

By the time you get to the bottom of five 'Whys' you either have clear strategic relevance or a senseless argument that completely discounts the 'should' in the first place.

You might not even get to the fifth 'Why' before recognizing that a 'should' has no strategic relevance.

For example

Henry always used to put on the menu 'gratuities included'.

■ *Why?*   Don't know. Impossible to answer.

CHALLENGING BEHAVIOUR

ACTIVITY 3 – GO BEYOND THE LIMITS

Give yourself a difficult time by honestly answering these questions:

- What would you endeavour to do if you knew you couldn't fail?
- What five key things might you do wrong that would result in the organization failing to meet its mission?

ACTIVITY 4 – STRATEGIC DOING

One of the biggest traps that you could fall into when you take on a new role requiring strategy development is to fall back into *doing* operational activities from your past. A discipline in strategic thinking is to stay with the discomforts of not doing; to recognize the different 'activities' in strategic thinking – rather than getting sucked back into the comfort zone of 'doing' what you know best.

Here are some actions that you and your team can engage in, that will contribute to strategic thinking:

- Keep space in your diary for *thinking* time.
- Be rigorous about keeping up to date with the local and national news.
- Be rigorous about keeping up to date with the organization's activities.

ACTIVITY 5 – NOTICING WHAT ISN'T BEING NOTICED

One of the skills of the strategic thinker is to notice what's in the 'space' between. So try:

- Seeing what isn't being seen
- Hearing what isn't being heard
- Saying what isn't being said.

CHALLENGING MANAGEMENT PERSPECTIVES

ACTIVITY 6 – ASKING QUALITY QUESTIONS

Quality questions get to the heart of the issue; particularly where people are concerned. A common error is to be passive, 'the service isn't very good'.

Try out a few ways of getting to the heart of the issue:

- What do *you* do that impedes the progress of . . . ?
- *Who* is responsible for supplying . . . on time?
- *What specifically can I do* to ensure the deadline is met?

ACTIVITY 7 – POLITICAL AWARENESS

When managers and teams find themselves taking on more of a strategic role, their ability to act politically becomes critical. Few organizations offer training in this area; people are expected to learn through personal insight and use others as a model for their own learning. Some achieve this, others continue in 'blissful naivety', then wonder why their career slowly comes to a halt, or the team fails to raise its profile.

Taking the idea that a message is only as good as the result it achieves:

- Reflect on a recent message you gave to someone or a group of people that did not achieve what you wanted. How could you have given that message to get a better result?
- Don't worry about the words so much, consider more about the process that you used, the situation you were in and your own behaviour at the time.
- Think of what has impact on others; who is the most influential person that would pass on your message to those whom you would wish to hear it; what 'currently fashionable' connections does your message link into; who are the right people to hear your message?

Political awareness is essential to your role as a strategist.

SUMMARY

To be completed by you and your team as a summary of your learning from these activities.

INTRODUCTION TO EMERGENT STRATEGY: THE ART OF STRATEGIC THINKING

PART 3

Emergent strategy itself implies learning what works ...
emergent strategy means, not chaos, but in essence unintended order.

Mintzberg and Waters (1985)

KEY LEARNING POINT
■ Understand four key attributes of emergent strategy

Ask almost anyone what strategy is and they will most likely describe it in terms of intentions; probably in terms of task intentions, where skills and abilities are easily defined and developed, just as in the first two sections of this book.

Emergent strategy could very easily be misinterpreted as a change in tactics on an intended journey by the persuasive pedlar. Do not be swayed. Emergent strategy is very different and much more profound than a simple tactical trick or opportunism.

There is no such thing a pure emerge strategy. It simply helps to define an develop the necessary skills if we carry the ide that such a concept is possible

EMERGENT STRATEGY DEFINED
The following definition is from *Collins English Dictionary*.
Emergent coming into being, arrival, appearing, budding, rising

For example

In my own garden, when new shoots grow I only
occasionally know the difference between plants and weeds.

I've reached a point where I'm never really sure what to call a weed anyway. Each season brings new intrigue and curiosity. I now have beautiful displays of buttercups along a bank in late spring and a wonderful show of flowering grasses that have seeded themselves in a little wooded area. I only pull out the plants that seem to try to take over. I look for balance and variety not by 'planting in' but by 'pulling out'. The art is not to pull shoots out too soon. I have trees which have grown through their own free will, ivy which throws tendrils down to the ground, and birds and animals that bring my garden to life. My garden has taken shape through an emergent process.

Now, in my neighbour's garden there isn't a buttercup in sight. Their garden is formal, planted in; intentional. Their planned garden suits them as much as my emergent garden suits me.

Emergent strategy is about allowing the unexpected to take place

Where determined strategy is about looking ahead – looking out, building on existing potential to achieve the goal – emergent strategy is about looking inward, allowing new ideas and unformed potential within the human system to take shape as they emerge.

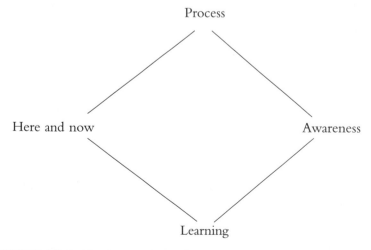

FIGURE P3.1 The four key attributes of emergent strategy

The attributes in Figure P3.1 together provide the essential requirements for developing an emergent approach to strategy formation:

- *Process* as the focus (not task)
- *Awareness* as a central theme
- *Learning* as the essence
- *Here and now* oriented (as opposed to futuristic).

Of greatest significance is the idea of working with a process, rather than a set of techniques. Although artists learn many techniques to develop their skills, ultimately when they put brush to canvas, pastels to sugar paper, hand to clay, the techniques flow through an interactive process between the artists and the subject of their work. I will briefly explain what I mean by these attributes.

PROCESS

Although emergent strategy is becoming increasingly popular as a working concept in developing strategy, very little has been achieved so far in defining the learning processes that aid the development of 'emergent skills'. These skills are *not* task skills, they are *process* skills. This lack of understanding I believe has led to a slow uptake in an increasingly important aspect of strategy formation, and organization functioning. Trying to practise emergent strategy through a task focus doesn't work.

Process in this context is a term that needs to be clarified for it has a specific meaning and must not be confused with task processes or operational procedures. What I am referring to is *personal process*. Personal processes are the mental and physical processes that occur within and between people. They generate our behaviour individually and collectively.

Through understanding these processes we can be choiceful in how we engage with the world; in the level of *contact* that we have with other people, situations and events; the physical and social environment around us. Read through the scenario given below. The words in italic define a process that is occurring.

Scenario – The meeting

When you meet a close friend you are likely to *make good contact immediately* and *engage in fairly intimate conversation spontaneously*. When you meet a stranger with whom you need to engage, you have to *make assumptions* about this person in order to begin developing a relationship. As you develop your relationship with them you consciously or unconsciously *continually check and revise your assumptions* until you find a point of good contact. You may continue this process for some time, depending on whether you wish the relationship to develop or not.

In this scenario, many blocks could prevent you from developing a healthy relationship with the stranger. For example, if in your assumptions you hold a prejudice towards this person then that will colour your 'check and revise' process. This type of block is discussed in more detail in Chapter 15.

Emergent strategy comes about through an active and engaging process, of which you are in control. It is not passive.

AWARENESS

To be able to respond effectively to an emergent process you will need an increased sense of awareness; to consciously observe your inner and outer world. Awareness is about making connections, noticing, collecting information, integrating, being in touch with the world around you and your responses to the environment.

Noticing shapes, form and patterns are at the core of emergent strategy. Putting yourself into an unknowing position, noticing the obvious, feeling at ease with ambiguity, allowing a process to unfold and to make sense of the unfolding, are characteristic behaviours in the art of strategic thinking. This process is non-casual and non-lineal. It is about turning science over to art.

LEARNING

Implicit in emergent strategy is learning. It is through engaging with learning, developing and building on learning, that patterns begin to form. Musicians who are composing a new piece of music do not start with the complete work already preformed in their minds, they take a theme and allow patterns to emerge. They experiment, put together sequences of sounds, bringing in harmony, rhythm, melody, pitch, patterns that go well together and seem fitting to the theme. The process is one of:

- Investigation
- Trial and error
- Experiment
- Testing
- Reflecting
- and learning.

Through allowing patterns to become concrete musicians will adjust, adapt, re-create until they reach a point of completion. Only then will they know what their final piece will really sound like.

In teams it is through people working together, learning from each other and their diverse responses to the environment that they move towards finding a common, often unexpected pattern that works for them; they are involved in co-creating.

HERE AND NOW

Unlike determined strategy which is futuristic, emergent strategy is much more about engaging with what is happening in 'this place and time'. This is not to say that reflections of the past and expectations of the future do not play a part in emergent strategy. That would contradict the principle of learning. It simply means that by paying attention to the present you are able to engage with the tensions from your reflections and expectations, in the context of your current reality. It is only through your current reality that the emergent process will take place and become realized – because you learn first hand.

These four attributes underpin the learning in the following three chapters.

Exercise 35 – Assess your skills and abilities on the four attributes of emergent strategy

To what level are these statements true for you, on a scale whereby 1 = not true at all and 7 = very true.

	Score from 1 to 7	What do you need to do to improve this skill/ability?
Process In team meetings I pay attention to the inter-actions between team members, as well as the points being discussed		
I draw on other team members' potential to achieve team success		
I know my limitations in my work		
I know the difference between good contact and bad conduct with the people I work with		
Awareness I have a good sense of self awareness		
I am a good listener		
I am aware of my prejudices		
Learning I always like to learn in every aspect of my work and my life		

I encourage others in their learning		
I know as much as I need to about different learning styles		
I work in an environment where learning is well supported		
I am able to experiment with new ideas and take risks in my work		
Here and now I pay a lot of attention to the current reality		
When discussions and behaviours are avoiding immediate issues I intervene to address them		

In the next three chapters you will have the opportunity to learn some skills to enable you and your team to work with emergent strategy. They are quite different to those which you have been exposed to so far and can be powerful in their application. These chapters are an introduction to the working practices of emergent strategy.

The final chapter brings emergent and determined strategy together.

CHAPTER 13 – LEARNING THE ART

In this chapter you will learn and practise the process skills needed for thinking strategically using an emergent approach.

CHAPTER 14 – FIELD VISION

Emergent strategy is not without vision. It is, however, different to moving towards a desired outcome. This chapter explores a new approach to visioning – an approach that particularly helps in times of change.

CHAPTER 15 – VALUING DIVERSE THINKING

The importance of respecting and valuing difference in people's thinking is where the creative process begins in emergent thinking. You and your team can learn how to embrace the diversity that exists around you and make the best of it.

CHAPTER 16 – DEVELOPING INTEGRATED STRATEGY

Now it is time to bring these two different perspectives for developing strategy together, to bring into being a dynamic way of thinking strategically that offers a powerful process for strategy formation.

FURTHER READING

For further reading you could refer to the work of Henry Mintzberg, Margaret Wheatley and to the philosophy and practice of Gestalt; some useful references are given at the back of this book. All three have influenced and inspired my practice in organizations and my writing in the following chapters.

CHAPTER 13

*L*EARNING THE ART

KEY LEARNING POINTS

- Understand 'letting go'
- Understand process skills
- Be able to increase awareness as a process of change
- Know how to use energy flows to your advantage

CREATING THE RIGHT ENVIRONMENT FOR PRACTISING EMERGENT STRATEGY

You can create an environment in which emergent strategies can grow, where learning is fostered. It means building flexible structures, loosening authoritative control, encouraging creativity and risk taking. Above all, it will mean allowing your team to learn from their mistakes and to squash destructive behaviours such as humiliation, blame or criticism. If your organization carries a culture where people are constantly watching their backs and praise is at a premium, it will be quite hard for your team to engage with emergent strategy.

Strategies can form as well as be formulated. Mintzberg (1987)

The role for you and your team will be to encourage relationships where people can learn and develop through each other's knowledge and expertise. Then, through your own curiosity and interest you should watch for patterns to emerge and harness them into 'possibilities' for strategy development.

THE NEED TO LET GO

Many organizations carry an obsession about leadership having the answers. This has come about largely because high degrees of uncertainty are *not* satisfying, therefore people seek answers in an attempt to regain a sense of comfort and control. This obsession for answers needs to be let go if emergent strategy is to find a place in the working practices of the organization. When demands are being made to find answers and to release discomforts about uncertainty, senior management must be able to say 'we don't know yet'; and middle management must be able to handle their senior managers' not knowing, and to feel okay about not knowing themselves.

This is a one-hundred-and-eighty-degree turn from the role that many managers and teams believe they need to play in order to be successful in their work and in their careers. The truth of the matter is that the world of business is also turning, calling for new practices. The growth of emergent strategy demands a radical shift, to let go of over-structured management and organizational practices, to bring in new, more fluid styles of operating.

Taking the risk of working with emergent processes need not start with huge steps of change. You have choice in the matter. You can choose to take little steps to start with, as you and your team learn and integrate the skills that you need to develop for working with emergent strategy.

PROCESS SKILLS

UNDERSTANDING PROCESS

Process is about how things happen, rather than what needs to

Process is about how things happen, rather than what needs to happen

happen. It requires a different attitude of mind. So, in a discussion the focus changes from the content of the discussion to the interaction between the people involved. In strategy formation it changes from what you are trying to achieve (determined), to how behaviour is influenced in order *to* achieve (emergent).

Process is implicit in the word emergent – something that is 'coming into being' is all process. When something comes into being, it is as though it has stepped out of the background, out of the hum and buzz of daily life and made its presence felt, gained our attention – it becomes *figure*, our awareness of it expands and we make meaning of it. This is like watching a picture from an instant camera develop. There is a point when we recognize the pattern in the picture, we start making sense of it, long before it is fully developed.

When you are paying attention to the process, the way you work with people becomes different. You notice how you interact as much, if not more than, what is being said or done. Have you ever walked away from a conversation with someone feeling uncomfortable, yet not knowing why? That is an under–processed picture. (Over-processing is when you leave the picture too long in the processing phase, for example where orderliness turns into analysis.)

> **When you are paying attention to the process, the way you work with people becomes different**

The idea that process is linked to *figure* that emerges out of *background* is not new (I refer the interested reader to Clarkson and Mackewn (1995) to gain a deeper understanding of this concept).

There is a third element which plays an important role in the processes of emergent strategy and a sense of coming into order. That is the significance of the *environmental field*. I will explain this further, using the photograph metaphor. The quality of the instant photograph is influenced by the conditions beyond the camera and emerging picture. There is the immediate impact of the weather conditions, the skills of the camera operator to bring the picture into focus, the subject matter, advancements in technology, the world economy and so on.

These are the *field conditions*; the interdependent factors of a person and their environment. I will expand on this concept in the next chapter, when you will look at visioning processes of emergent strategy.

Exercise 36 – Figuring it all out!

This exercise will lead to a better understanding of the concept of figure, ground and field.

Scenario – The day Henry died

As Henry lay on his death bed he spoke briefly to Caroline before he died. Through her grief she heard him say 'I want you to keep the restaurant going, I've left it all to you in my will'. Caroline was shocked. She knew he was dying, but had he known all the time that he was going to die so early in his life? Anyway, how could she keep the restaurant going, she had her own career to follow? How would she cope? She let her thoughts drop as he gave out one last sigh.

She sat in a daze, holding his hand, until she noticed it growing cold. Somehow it seemed appropriate that the smell of French cooking was wafting in through the window on that summer's day.

From the scenario above, get your team to identify the following components of the interaction between Caroline and her father, bringing in their knowledge of the scenario so far.

- What figures emerge and recede?
- Describe the ground out of which these figures emerge.
- What are the field conditions that influence this interaction?

Discuss with your team the conclusions you have come to and raise further questions that might lead to greater clarity of this often confusing concept.

In every situation you are in, like now, these three aspects of process – figure, ground and field – exist. Good skills practice would be to stop in your work at any moment of the day and define them in that present moment.

AWARENESS

Awareness is the process of making sense of figures that are emerging, that is, ideas, imaginings, perceptions, sounds, feelings and so on. The most fundamental of all process skills in emergent strategy lies in developing an acute sense of awareness and awareness raising skills.

We all have the capacity to keep our awarenesses out of reach if we perceive them to cause us discomfort. In so doing we prevent change. Process skills include surfacing discomforts to promote change, as well as surfacing people's potential and ideas.

Forcing an emerging figure to take shape too soon can distort it. This can happen in times of change when people feel uncomfortable with 'not knowing'. Pushing the flow forward is about taking over control; allowing the flow to find its natural path is staying with the discomfort until the figure emerges enough to be recognizable. This is a different sort of control and is illustrated in the following scenario.

Scenario – Trusting the process

After Henry died, Caroline entrusted the staff of the restaurant with the job of keeping it going until she could get a sense of her own direction. To start with they were very willing to help out, but after six weeks and still no idea of what Caroline's intentions were they started to get edgy. Every time Caroline came into the restaurant they expected her to say something. Caroline would apologize for the delay and ask them to wait. She just said she needed time.

Caroline was holding back, rather than diving into action. She needed to know for herself, despite her father's wishes, that the responsibility she was taking on was what she wanted to do. After all, she could have sold the restaurant. Holding back until she was absolutely clear that she was doing the right thing paid off. Once she made her decision she plunged wholeheartedly into turning the restaurant into a business success ... and she intended to do it differently to the way her father had worked.

If Caroline had moved too soon, to ease both her own discomforts and those of the staff, she might have made the wrong decision and regretted it for a long time.

CLOSING DOWN TOO SOON

One final point before you move on is related to conversations. In my experience many people *close down* too soon in their conversations. There are still too many gaps that they have to fill in order to establish a pattern; of gaining good understanding. When this happens they fill the gaps with their own values, beliefs, thoughts, perceptions, past experiences, assumptions and so on. You can avoid this trap by increasing your awareness of how you engage in and end conversations.

INCREASING AWARENESS

Awareness is the key to experiment and change. The following behaviours will help increase your awareness:

- Notice what is missing rather than what is present, that is, feelings, topics, information, enthusiasm, congruence and so on.
- Detect patterns and themes in your interactions, saying what you notice.
- Bring your curiosity into your work.
- Scan as well as focus on your environment – develop your peripheral vision.
- *Really* hear what others have to say.
- Notice things in wholes as well as their fragments.
- Amplify difference.

- Notice how you block your awareness, for instance:
  - Talking too much
  - Criticism and cynicism
  - Your own preoccupations
  - Avoidance
  - Pushing for your ideas to be observed.

Exercise 37 – Team awareness

Head up three flip charts with the following:

ESTABLISHED AWARENESS RAISING BEHAVIOURS
NEW AWARENESS RAISING BEHAVIOURS
AWARENESS BLOCKING BEHAVIOURS

Then invite your team to do the following exercise.

As you do this exercise pay attention to the awareness raising behaviours listed above. You will learn best by engaging *in* process skills as well as increasing your understanding through discussion.

Established awareness raising behaviours
Identify all the awareness raising activities that you already engage in either as individuals or collectively.

New awareness raising behaviours
Develop your own ideas of awareness raising activities. As ideas emerge share them. If they don't fit, reject them.

Awareness blocking behaviours
Go round the team and identify individual behaviours that block awareness, at least two for every team member. Then note five blocks that the group collectively engage in.

- Are there patterns which emerge from this exercise?
- What do you notice?
- What is missing?

FOLLOWING ENERGY FLOWS

In her work the artist engages with the energy of her subject and allows it to flow through her. This helps her create images on her canvas. Patterns form through connecting her own energy with life around her.

Energy flows are invisible to the naked eye, silent to the ear, tasteless to the tongue, untouchable to the finger and odourless to the nose. Yet we know they exist, they are all around us, they are in nature, in ourselves; we *sense* them. For example, the ghostly atmosphere of an old ruin throwing shadows in the moonlight; the excitement of a babbling brook on a cold spring morning; the silence of a post–lunch period as the teacher wades through a heavy curriculum.

It is through developing the senses that can detect *changes* in energy flows that you and your team will increase your ability to work well with emergent strategy. Your role, after all, is two-fold:

1. To create an environment in which ideas and innovation can emerge.
2. To follow energy flows, rather than swim against the tide, in order to notice, discover and encourage the converging of ideas in the work place.

It is the latter of these that we look at here.

Working with energy flows in an organization can be likened to a river; that is:

- Convergence of streams
- Divergence of rivers
- Surface ripples
- Undertows
- Waterfalls and whirlpools
- Dangerous rapids
- Soft and flowing estuaries
- Full of flotsam and jetsam after a storm
- Drying up to a trickle after a drought
- Always winding its way forward as though aware of its destination, but not knowing.

> ... it [convergence] just evolves through a host of individual actions ... more from collective action than intention. Mintzberg and Waters (1985)

To try and swim against the flow is draining of energy, and often fruitless – unless you happen to be a salmon in the spawning season! Following energy flows can lead the strategist to rich 'feeding grounds'.

When I am working in organizations I also pay attention

to the layers of energy. These layers change from individuals to teams to departments to the whole organization. There is usually a thread that runs through them all, and then there are individual energies that I pay particular attention to.

I have often found good productive energy of individuals held back, locked in like a bird in a cage, usually due to tight managerial control. My task has been to seek ways of releasing it without undermining the stability of the organization.

I notice the way people hold in or release their potential through their behaviour. Sometimes it is as simple as noticing their breathing. Other times it is just listening to the excitement of conversations on the grapevine. In this way I can see, hear, taste, touch and smell energy, as well as using my sixth sense. Such practice is frequently ignored in organizations, it is not seen to be important to strategic thinking. It is vitally important to emergent strategy, for it is in the 'field of energy' that ideas emerge, converge and become ordered.

Exercise 38 – Releasing energy

With your team create a metaphor that encompasses the energy streams in your organization, similar to my use of a river above. Then:

1. Define some attributes of this metaphor (about 10 to 15 examples).
2. If your metaphor describes difficulties, consider what these attributes mean in terms of blocking the energy flow. If your metaphor generates positive attributes, find where blocks could hinder the flow.
3. Give examples of what you can do to help unblock energy.

An example is given in the following table, based on the river metaphor.

Metaphor:	The energy flow is very strong, but like the slightly stagnant, dark foreboding of a river. Slow and deep. Difficult to manage	
Attributes	**What it might mean**	**What can you do?**
1. *Murky water*	*One part of the organization can't see what another is doing*	*Look for ways to clarify information about the organization*
2. *Gentle undertow*	*People are seductively dragged down into the organization and carried along helplessly*	*Encourage people to make a contribution, to stand out. Give them something to hold on to*
3. *Deep quiet pools*	*Parts of the organization are full of potential, but quiet and inactive*	*Stir up some movement. Throw a big stick in and try to get a response*
4. *Powerful*	*You know that a lot could be achieved by the very size of the organization and the force which must exist within it*	*Look for ways to build a generator. Talk to people about what power the organization has to achieve something*
5. *Not much birdlife*	*The river isn't attractive. It can't get new life*	*Decide how the organization can be made attractive. What would a potential recruit like to find?*
6. *Weeds are beginning to build up*	*Bureaucracy is beginning to slow the organization down. Achieving the simplest movement seems to be a fight*	*Clear the weeds. Have a specific campaign to rid areas of unnecessary systems, forms, procedures, rules*
7. *Very few visitors to the river*	*If anglers are customers then we're in some difficulty*	*How can we make it attractive, comfortable and worthwhile for the angler/customer?*
8. *Can't see any fish*	*The product is not visible enough*	*... and so on*
9.		

Identify how you might become more aware of energy in your everyday work, what you might notice and how you could intervene to release positive energy from the people around you.

For example

Organizations
- Excited chatter around the coffee machines – good feeding ground
- Long corridors and closed doors – energy and ideas held in
- Lots of energy going into computers, e-mail systems, little coming out.

Teams
- Little engagement with each other – fragmented energy, little chance of convergence of ideas
- You should begin to develop relationships.

Individuals
- Energy held in – silence, holding breath, clenched hands
- You should reveal your observations and responses to this held-in energy.

As you observe and intervene you will almost certainly detect patterns and connections between the organization's energy, the team's energy and individual energies. The forces between these interact. It is in the releasing of these energies that self organization occurs and unintended order (not chaos) is established.

- In doing this exercise notice the different energies in your team right now. Describe each member of your team in terms of how you perceive their energy and offer an observation, or sense, that has led you to this conclusion.
- When you have done this, in your team consider how you might change your working practice if you paid more attention to these energy flows.
- Discuss together how your increased awareness of energy flows will influence your strategic thinking.

SUMMARY

In this chapter you have had a glimpse of the art of emergent strategy; the underpinning of the skills around process. The process referred to here is predominantly based on expanding and furthering awareness. Increased awareness in itself creates movement and change.

As you may have realized, the more you discover the more there is to discover. That is because human behaviour is at the core of emergent processes and that collective behaviour plays such a big part in harnessing emerging ideas.

You need only a few skills to begin thinking and working with emergent strategy; more important is a sense of human nature and a good understanding of yourself. No doubt you and your team have many established skills already; it is just a matter of harnessing them in the right way.

There are many more skills to build on, too numerous to mention here. You will find more in the following two chapters which focus on visioning and diversity in emergent strategy, respectively.

CHAPTER 14

FIELD VISION

'I have come to understand organizational vision as a field – a force of unseen connections that influences employees' behaviour – rather than as an evocative message about some desired future state.

Wheatley (1992)

KEY LEARNING POINTS

- Understand the concept of field vision
- Understand the importance of self-organizing systems and their influence on field vision
- Be able to build quality contact in relationships
- Know how to develop a theme

During the late 1980s, many organizations had to let go of their long-term deterministic visions. They discovered that to navigate through a recession, strong core values and purpose (attributes of field vision) provided the basis for their decision making.

This indicates that we already *know* how to work with field vision, and in realizing this discover that human behaviour is central to the process. It is just that bringing the idea of field vision into our awareness makes us feel like it is new. Both the language and the concept seem new. At an intellectual level they may be; at an intuitive level they are not. As with all new ideas and concepts, we can feel incompetent to start with before we have had time to put them into practice and feel comfortable with them.

Recall the account of my garden at the beginning of this section, where I described an emergent process, or the idea of a musician creating a new musical composition. These are not without vision, albeit that the vision is different to the one with which you are familiar in determined strategy. It is field vision.

A *field* is not empty space. On the contrary it is filled with a richness of life and influenced by a complex web of interactions. My garden was not empty before I started, it was already full — an intricate web of interactions between animal life, plant life and the changing weather conditions. The changing shape of my garden has been influenced by my field vision of a natural garden. This vision was not a fixed end point by design, but a process of emerging ideas and inspiration which arrived through interacting with nature. A key attribute of field vision is the *collective* aspect of what emerges — a convergence of ideas.

Vision is an essential part of strategic thinking and organizational change processes. The vision in emergent strategy consists of abstract patterns and connections, rather than concrete images of the future. For example, it is not possible to have a concrete vision of a 'learning organization' — a learning organization emerges through a process of discovery, connections and influences. In this case the central *theme* is 'learning', in another case the theme will be different. The theme is connected to the notion of 'a wide ranging pattern of possibilities' for the outcome.

Both *theme* and *quality relationships* are enabling factors for strategy. They enable *self organization* to occur, which in turn generates emergent strategy. This is not a linear cause and effect process, but a complex, interactive system. The skill lies in noticing connections in your work and allowing yourself to experience an emergent process.

THE HEALTHY SELF-ORGANIZING SYSTEM

What if we stopped looking for control and began in earnest to search for order?
Wheatley (1992)

HAVE WE CONFUSED CONTROL WITH ORDER?

In nature we see, time and time again, examples of self-organizing systems. We have only to observe how quickly new growth returns after a bank fire on the edge of the motorway, to recognize nature's urgency for self organization. The capacity to learn and adjust in relation to the changing environment is paramount. The organization is a living system that has the capacity to self organize.

The conventional view of strategic development in organizations does not embrace this idea. A dependency is set up within the system that leads to people at the top dictating the direction of the business, rather than allowing the business to find its own direction through experiment, learning and inquiry. Conventionally, the drive to establish stability through control overrides the search for order. We are not familiar with staying with confusion until order emerges – traditionally, we are more familiar with getting organized through intention and planned action, rather than allowing self organization to occur.

Getting organized often denies the opportunity for new ideas. This does not mean 'let it all hang out and see what happens!' On the contrary, that is not how nature works and that is not how emergent strategy works. Nature is not passive in its survival and growth, it is an active participant in its own self-organizing system – as we need to be active participants in our own self-organizing systems. The process for this is inquiry – learning through investigation.

Nature is an active participant in its own self-organizing system – as we need to be active participants in our own self-organizing systems

We have advantage over much of nature through our intelligence. Yet intellect often wins over intelligence in the business world. The following definitions are from *Collins English Dictionary*.

Intellect   The capacity for understanding *thinking and reasoning*
Intelligence   The capacity for *understanding*. The ability to perceive and comprehend *meaning*

Intelligence means using *all* human faculties, not just those associated with thought and intellect. Using our intelligence wisely is at the core of self organization in business. Acting intelligently means responding to internal needs as well as external stimuli. By this, I mean both personally and organizationally. So, for example, if the organization is showing a high level of stress and sickness, operating only at a level of intellect, you might bring in a stress management programme to deal with the symptoms. Working intelligently would lead you to listen to the voice of the employees and let them tell you the source of their stress and what their real need is in order to deal with the cause.

To sum up, developing emergent strategy means:

■ That you need to actively engage in nurturing relation-ships and contacts within your organizational systems.

■ That you need to respond to your internal needs and the environment with intelligence – using your intellect as one of your resources.

ORDER

There is another aspect of the work that you and your team will need to consider. Moving forward through a self-organizing system means that control has to be different to working with structure and planned actions. The emphasis in a self-organizing system should be that of seeking *order*, not control as it is understood in a good many organizations. Order implies something taking shape, finding its own structure and pattern in a way that connects with the environment in which it forms. As Margaret Wheatley says, 'Order we will find in many places we never thought to look'.

> All this time we have created trouble for ourselves by confusing control with order. Wheatley (1992)

Field vision is self perpetuating, it creates order and self organization through the process of influence. We have seen this happen through bringing purpose and core values into the work place – these permeate the organization and influence the culture in a positive and productive way.

Order can be established by building *quality relationships* and developing *themes*.

QUALITY RELATIONSHIPS

Scenario – The medical profession as an art

In the medical profession today some medical practitioners will look for patterns in patients to inform the diagnosis, prognosis and treatment plan, rather than be too prescriptive and go straight to cause and effect cures. They treat each patient individually and don't assume that scientific research can give an immediate answer as to how to treat each particular patient. They will, however, use patterns in scientific research to provide information. An important aspect of this lies in developing a relationship with their patients so that the patients can also contribute to their own treatment. Practitioner and patient learn from each other. That can be an incredibly powerful process.

In order to discover these patterns, medical practitioners must be able to engage well with their patients; that means in a relationship where the power of the interaction is in balance, for example, without intimidation or becoming patronizing. Where there is mutual respect there is quality contact.

Where there is mutual respect, there is quality contact
(see Chapter 3)

Quality relationships in organizations can be generated in a range of ways. Coaching and mentoring draws out the best in many employees. So, too, does encouraging people to ask questions, to raise their curiosity and tap into their inquiring minds, to stimulate (not force) their taste buds for knowledge, understanding, innovation and creativity. Above all, you should encourage connections and good contactful working relationships, where challenge and support, rather than blame and shame, form the attitude for learning and moving forward. This culture will then offer important enablers for emergent strategy; for discovering the diversity of thought and converging of ideas.

MAKING GOOD CONTACT

Real contact leads to change. We know when we have made good contact – when we leave we feel different, in a way that indicates something has happened that wasn't there before. Yet good contact is surprisingly rare in many organizations. When I raise the subject in my work with managers and their teams, their response is often 'we don't have the time or energy'. In truth, it probably takes less time and energy than the cliché talk that many people engage in; although, of course, new encounters might take a period of time to get past the cliché stage of their relationship development.

So what do we mean when we refer to 'good contact'? In essence it is about treating *how* you interact with as much importance as the content of your interaction. The following four principles will help you and your team build good contactful relationships with the people that you work with, and with your customers.

1   INCLUSION

Bring yourself into the dialogue and include the other person as much as possible, without value judgement or premature analysis of what they say.

Reducing contact might sound like this: 'This has to be sorted out. Everyone here is so busy, but I suppose it'll only take a moment'. Increasing contact would sound like this: 'I need to sort this out. Are you able to help me? (*time for response*) How long do you think we could spend on this?' In the latter statement you own the problem and invite the other person to help you with it (inclusion of both yourself and them), as well as constructively addressing the time issue.

2   THE THIRD ENTITY

Choosing to increase contact between you and the other person/people leads to the development of a third entity. The third entity is the relationship and can be described in terms of the nature of the relationship, e.g. friend, colleague, parent. It can also be described in terms of the quality of the relationship, e.g. intimate, trusting, conflicting and so on.

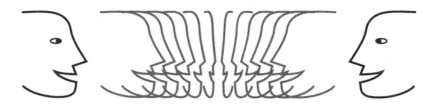

FIGURE 14.1 The existence of a third entity

Although difficult to illustrate visually, Figure 14.1 indicates the existence of a third entity.

If the third entity does not exist, you may feel like you don't exist for the other person.

3 LIVING THE DIALOGUE

Many people spend endless time talking 'about' what they feel and believe in, rather than living out their feelings. Like a colleague of mine who was telling me about a past incident in which she had felt angry with me. She talked about it as though she was no longer angry, that her anger had been 'there and then'. Yet her tone of voice indicated that this was not true. I said, 'You sound as though you are still angry with me'. My comment seemed to make it safe for her to show her anger, rather than skirt around it – she was able to live it and deal with the issue directly. It was a rich and contactful discussion that ensued.

4 CONGRUENCE

Being congruent in your conversations with people leads to good contact because people trust what you say. Incongruence blocks contact. Most people sense incongruence through discomforts, often not knowing what their discomfort is about.

- *Congruence* is when your language and behaviour are aligned.
- *Incongruence* is when you say one thing and behave in a way that does not support what you are saying; for example stating 'I am angry with you' with a smile on your face.

You need to have a good sense of self awareness in order to be fully congruent in your interactions with others.

There are many skills for improving contact in your relationships at work and in your life. These are just a few examples.

Exercise 39 – Making contact

Working in pairs, get your team to choose one of the four topics for making good contact:

- Inclusion
- The third entity
- Living the dialogue
- Congruence

Their task is to design a short activity or presentation (which will take no longer than five minutes) which will help the rest of the team understand each topic more fully. Allow about 10 minutes for the pairs to design this activity, then run them through.

In your review of this exercise, ask your team 'What new learning has this exercise given you in relation to developing strategy?'

Exercise 40 – Qualities of good contact

This exercise will expand your team's awareness of many other contact behaviours that they notice within the team and work place.

Now that they are getting a sense of the difference between good contact and diminished contact, ask your team to make a list on the sheet below of all the behaviours which they see around them in the team and their work place. They should be specific.

Contact and behaviours	
Blocks to contact	**Contactful behaviours**
Everyone agreed with the decision at the client meeting, then immediately complained afterwards	*Bob revealed that he was having difficulty in understanding my e-mail messages*

BUILDING ON A THEME

The definition below is from *Collins English Dictionary*.

Theme A unifying idea (repeated or developed throughout a work of art, music or literature)

A theme captures the essence of the vision, permeating through the whole organization; like the theme of a song that carries through from beginning to end. You may recall a favourite piece of music that has been played many times on many instruments with many interpretations – the theme is never lost. People associate with it and remember it.

The theme plays a number of important functions in field vision and emergent strategy.

1. Themes emerge from a self-organizing system – they are *not put into* the system.
2. Themes are carried through the system and influence the direction of change.
3. The unifying attributes of a theme provide important stability in changing environments.
4. A theme can express itself in many ways.
5. Theme is an attribute of the field and also influences the field.

Let's look at these functions in the context of an organization. The numbers in the scenario relate to the numbers of the functions listed above.

Scenario – The Engineering Company

The Engineering Company had been manufacturing cars for several years based on a deterministic strategic approach. As competition increased The Engineering Company's sales decreased, until the decline began to cause grave concerns.

The management finally called all the employees together, declared the severity of their problem and asked for help. They no longer believed that their traditional strategic approach would shift them out of crisis. They informed the employees that a new radical approach was needed and that they would work closely with the employees to find a new direction that would shift them out of crisis. The employees were now empowered to rescue their own jobs. The management had put an *enabling factor* into the organizational system nudging it into a self-organizing process (1).

During the following weeks the management and staff met frequently in various ways. Employees formed 'rescue' groups. Contrary to the management's predictions a lively buzz seemed to permeate the buildings.

Eventually the staff came up with an obvious solution (**1**). Their real leading edge skills were in designing engines – out of which cars were manufactured. Why not concentrate the organization's energy around this theme, by *producing all sorts of different engines* rather than continuing to re-invent the car? As soon as this idea emerged it was taken as a theme for change. Both management and employees set about building on their theme (**3**). People bounced ideas off each other, particularly focusing on the skill base that existed; some ideas came and went, others were developed (**5**).

The skill base offered numerous possibilities. They started branching out into engines for lawn mowers, garden machinery, motor bikes, portable generators and small agricultural equipment (**4**). One idea led to another (**2**). The business not only survived but it became a leading manufacturer in many of these areas.

Once a theme exists and infiltrates the whole organization, people meet it wherever they go, bumping into it in all sorts of places. It provides order to the field vision which then generates change.

Exercise 41 – Chasing a theme

Your team can now explore together the restaurant scenario. Basing their discussion on what they know about the restaurant, get them to:

1. Describe three specific enablers which they could introduce into the system that would create a self-organizing system.
2. Imagine that they are the restaurant staff (chef, kitchen staff, waitress, wine waiter, administrator, gardener, cleaner and so on) thrown into chaos by Henry's death. They should build on what they know already about the life of the restaurant. Then

ask them to name five different themes that they consider might emerge.

3. Take two of these themes. How do they think each theme would influence the future developments of the restaurant? What differences and similarities emerge from the two themes?

SUMMARY

Field vision is about thinking in terms of processes rather than tangible outcomes. This isn't to say that tangible outcomes are not achieved – The Engineering Company clearly achieved a very tangible productive outcome. Allowing a vision to emerge means firstly kicking the system into self organization. In today's terms, this involves throwing in enabling forces that create positive energy within the system. We visited a number of enablers in this chapter, but there are many, too numerous to mention. You will probably have discovered more already. The principle to bear in mind for the strategist is that you *enable*.

CHAPTER 15

VALUING DIVERSE

THINKING

Nothing really transfers: everything is always new and different and unique to each of us.

Wheatley (1992)

KEY LEARNING POINTS
- Understand the importance of diverse thinking
- Know how to differentiate in order to integrate ideas
- Be able to surface and manage prejudices

Can you just imagine what it would be like if we were all the same?

Exercise 42 – Same or different?

Before you begin to explore and discuss the meaning of diverse thinking in emergent strategy, involve your team in the following exercise:

1. As a member of this team, imagine that everyone in the team

is the same as you in their personality, behaviour, values, beliefs, abilities, talents, attitudes, outlook on life, skills, ambitions and so on. Allow this experience to linger, notice what is good about it and what is not good about it. Make a note of these.

2. When you have done this, do the opposite. Imagine that you are all completely different, so different that it seems you have never met people 'like this' before. You have nothing to compare them with.

   Once again, allow this experience to linger. Notice what happens to you – are you curious, scared, shy, inquisitive? Do you want to find out about the other people and tell them about yourself, or are you shy and withholding, reluctant to engage? Write down your thoughts and experiences.

3. Discuss your thoughts and experiences. You might like to bring in the following questions:
   - What are the messages that come out of this exercise for you in relation to emergent strategy?
   - What does this exercise tell you about how you work as a team?
   - In the second part of the exercise did you start trying to 'make meaning' of some people?

In this chapter diversity means 'where people are different to each other'.

Many organizational cultures encourage conformity, bringing out people's similarities rather than their differences. A fear of rejection stops people from showing their differences. This is unfortunate in that the organization denies its capacity to draw on the potential in the diversity of the workforce. It is within this diversity that emergent strategy is really able to exist. In diversity there is novelty and novelty evokes excitement and interest. In extremely conforming organizations, it is unlikely that emergent strategy will find a place to come alive. Emerging processes are somewhat dependent on an environment that encourages (or even rewards) different styles of thinking, a wide variety of working practices and a good range of different behaviours.

This is a very large topic area, so I have selected three particularly significant subjects within diversity that I refer to as the *3Ds*. They will help you and your team begin a process of development in this area:

- Discovering
- Differentiating
- Discriminating.

THE 3DS

DISCOVERING

Exercise 43 – Meeting diversity

Moving on from the second part of Exercise 42, you have been told that you and this group of 'different' people actually have one or two things in common. For example, you can speak a common language and, between you, you have all that it takes to make your business succeed – a restaurant.

Get your team to:

1. Discuss what would be the first steps that you could take towards developing your business.
2. Write up on a flip chart things which might get in the way and ruin your chances of success.

Discuss the outcome of this exercise with your team, asking them where they feel most comfortable, for example with people who are:

- *Different* therefore they stand out.
- *Similar* therefore they feel a sense of belonging.

What issues on the flip chart do you see occurring in your real place of work?

Valuing difference is an important skill in any business environment because it opens up possibilities, rather than closing down on them before they surface. Yet it often takes unusual conditions and situations to help people see that the richness of diversity exists.

One reason for this is that the need to belong is very powerful for most people. To be valued and appreciated is generally linked to belonging and conforming, rather than to difference. For a number of reasons diversity frequently leads to humiliation and isolation in organizations – experiences that many people fear. No wonder we lose sight of the colourful tapestry of diversity at work; it goes underground.

Discovering and valuing the many experiences, talents and wisdom that people bring to the work place is a task that the strategic thinker will need to undertake. The richness of emergent strategy lies within people, just like it does within the artist. Without tapping into this richness the artist only has a set of tools and techniques. The emerging work of art not only loses its soul, it also loses the richness of the artist's life experiences, and the very special, individual lens through which they see the world. Discovering:

- Is being open and receptive; not closed and defensive.
- Is being curious, as though you are meeting the world for the first time.
- Means valuing other people with different perspectives to your own and accepting that both yours and theirs are valid.
- Means letting go, or loosening rigid beliefs.
- Means respecting different viewpoints even though you might not agree with them.
- Means inviting others in.

Through working in this way emergent strategy has already harnessed within it the tapestry of colour that exists in the work place. Your task will be to let patterns and connections fully emerge, even if you end up discarding some of them along the way. Let's reflect back on the restaurant as an example of losing out through lack of respect for difference.

DISCOVERING INTUITION
Opposite is the lifeline of the restaurant, repeated from Chapter 7.

The lifeline indicated the difficulties that Henry had experienced with the business over the years. If Henry had followed an emergent strategy through times of change and difficulty, it might have been that he would have come

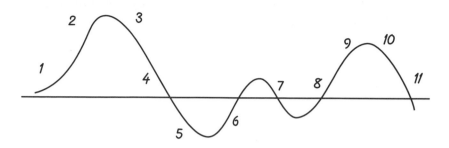

FIGURE 15.1 Restaurant customer graph

through those difficulties more productively. As it happened, his staff were not involved and Henry struggled on single-mindedly, 'determined' to achieve *his* goals.

Henry did not seek to discover difference. For example, he did not value intuitive thinking, he demanded decisions supported by logical reasoning. Had he listened to his head chef leading up to the beef crisis, who intuitively suggested that they have a 'special' promotion of vegetarian food, the restaurant would probably not have slumped in the way that it did.

He might even have lived longer by reducing his stress, had he discovered and drawn on the diversity of his staff – but that is by-the-by.

Seeking difference can lead to validating different behaviours simply because you begin to see their success on a regular basis and in a different light. Unknown to Henry the head chef operated predominantly on an intuitive basis very successfully, but because Henry demanded logic the chef would produce the evidence needed to support his actions, often after the event. So Henry never gave himself the opportunity to validate intuition as a useful style of operating.

THE SPIRIT OF TALKING ABOUT: STORY TELLING AS A MEANS OF DISCOVERING DIVERSITY

Scenario – Mark's story telling session

Mark sat in the room with his mother and the rest of the staff. Having made the decision to change his career path he was energized to make the restaurant a success with his mother. He knew that the best way to move forward would be to hear from all the staff – and that they all heard each other. Through this he felt that between them they could begin to build a picture. He said, 'Tell me what it has been like working here for you since you started'. One by one they spontaneously 'told their story', each one of them different, albeit that many had similar experiences. Mark and Caroline also told their stories of their associations with the restaurant, indicating that they had found their father difficult at times, even though they dearly loved him.

In listening to each story, Mark followed three simple rules:

1. *To hear each story without question or judgement.*
2. *To be revealing of his own personal response (observations – what was missing as well as what he noticed – imaginings and emotions) to each story.* For example, when one of the waitresses talked about the layout of the tables and how Henry had been adamant that they remain fixed, Mark said 'I imagine that has been quite difficult for you at times when serving customers'. This resulted in the waitress revealing how it had been difficult for her, how it had led to occasional accidents, and offering what she thought would be a much better layout.
3. *To expand upon the stories by reflecting on 'high energy spots' in the telling.* For example, when the head chef commented that he had felt very constrained by Henry, Mark noticed a change in his voice. When the chef had finished talking,

Mark referred back to the comment, inviting him to expand on what he had meant by this and how he would have liked it to have been.

Using these three rules Mark was able to ensure that stories were told 'from the heart', which would be informative in many ways. In particular, he was able to detect a *theme* throughout all of them which would inform his strategic thinking. As it happened, he discovered two themes:

1 Discontented staff.
2. A deep desire to contribute to the 'life', rather than the 'death', of the restaurant.

I spoke earlier of the importance of engaging with the present, the here and now. Story telling might seem contradictory to this function, because it is talking about 'there and then', yet the value really lies in how the story is told in the present.

When engaging in story telling exercises people often ask me 'where do I start?, 'where does my story begin – out there or in here, within me?' As it happens, it doesn't matter, both are relevant, you can't have one without the other. You start where you need to start.

Exercise 44 – Story telling

There are a number of ways to engage in story telling. Three possibilities are:

■ Simply as a narrative, like Mark did with his staff.
■ Through *faction*, that is, through combining facts with inventive fiction.
■ To tell the story as it *wasn't* rather than as it was – this can be fun and quite revealing.

Select one of these options and then decide on a topic relevant to your team. This might range from a recent experience with a customer/supplier to what it has been like as a member of this team/organization since you joined. There are many possibilities, but it is best that you use the same topic for everyone in this exercise.

Share with your team the three rules that Mark used. These

are very important for the recipient when they are listening to another person's story.

Working in pairs, starting with one person telling their story and the other listening, allow 10 minutes for the story and 10 minutes for the recipient to share their response and expand on 'hot spots'. Then swap round.

You could, of course, also do this exercise all together as long as your group or team isn't too large.

In your review discuss the following:

- What it was like to be able to tell a story and be listened to.
- What it was like for recipients to practise the rules (skills) and what they discovered which was new.
- How you might naturally engage in such an exercise in the 'flow of conversation', rather than as a structured entity.
- What themes did you notice, were there patterns emerging between stories?
- How such an exercise could contribute to emergent strategy.

> Strategy is spontaneously emerging from the chaos of challenge and contradiction through a process of real time learning and politics.
> Stacey (1993)

DIFFERENTIATING

When people show their individuality and their special talents and skills are valued in the work place then good differentiation is present. However, organizational cultures tend to respect and value similarities rather than build on difference. As a consequence people merge together; they become confluent like two rivers merging. After a while, difference is less visible and similarities more apparent. A simple illustration in Figure 15.2 demonstrates this point.

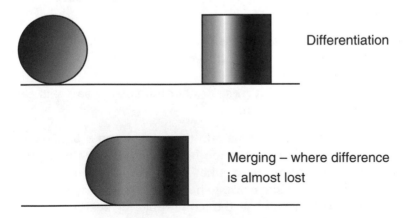

Differentiation

Merging – where difference is almost lost

FIGURE 15.2 Merging of difference

When difference is lost, novelty and interest are also lost. There is little opportunity for new and fresh ideas to come to the surface.

The first exercise in this chapter addressed the polarities of *extreme difference* and *extreme similarities* and the effect on us when we lean into one or the other. Such extremes do not support emergent strategy. The point I am making is that where there is a high imbalance it will disturb the possibility of a good emergent process occurring. Usually this imbalance is towards similarity rather than difference, although in some industries the opposite does occur.

DISCOVERING DIFFERENCE

When you look around, you can see difference from which you will make assumptions – some assumptions may be true, most will not be true. What you cannot do is see the difference in the way people think, you can only see their behaviour and make your assumptions from this. Shown in Figure 15.3 is a water line. Above the water line are the behaviours that are accessible to us; we see and we hear. Below the water line are the many aspects of human process that are only accessible through behaviour and language; we cannot see or hear them. We only know our own processes. These processes, then, are what we make assumptions about. Its no wonder that human interaction is open to error and mis-interpretation!

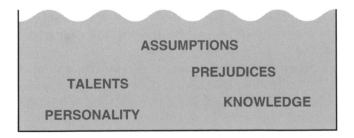

FIGURE 15.3 The hidden processes

There are only a few aspects of human process identified in Figure 15.3. The following exercise will allow you and your team to identify many more.

Exercise 45 – The water line

Draw the diagram in Figure 15.3 on a flip chart.

Add as many hidden human processes and attributes as you can think of which exist below the water line. See how many you can come up with.

Discovering hidden difference that exists below the water line requires good contact with people. That is one reason why spending time developing relationships is so important. The more you engage with people, the more you and they will differentiate. You will see each other for what you really are, rather than through assumptions, stereotyping, judging and so on. In this process you might either reject or value the difference that you see. One of the most difficult things for most people to do is value difference when it is a complete polar opposite to your own way of operating and thinking. Psychometric tests have brought this to our awareness and helped people learn how to appreciate rather than reject difference. Psychometric tests, however, have their limitations.

Exercise 46 – Same or different?

One way of dealing with this problem is very simple – seek out opposites and similarities. With your team working in pairs, ask them to write down all the attributes that are similar between themselves and the other person, then all the attributes that are different. They should identify at least 10 of each and, staying in the pairs, share them. If you have time you could then get them to move on to another pair and repeat the same exercise.

People sometimes get stuck in how they *should* be doing the exercise. There is no fixed rule, no right or wrong, your opinion and viewpoint might be different to others; that is all right, too. Just follow your flow of thinking.

Having done this exercise myself I realize that it isn't as easy as it seems. However, once I had got used to thinking in this way I realized that I could do it all the time, pointing out to my colleagues when I noticed new similarities and differences as they came to light. Over time this has become very productive in many ways.

DISCRIMINATING

Collins English Dictionary gives the following definitions:

Discrimination   The ability to see fine distinctions and differences
Discrimination   ... action based on prejudice

Already in this section you will notice that there is a problem. The very term that offers the strategic thinker some direction in their skills development – *to see fine distinctions and differences* – also creates the very blocks which might stop them from discovering valuable and important differences – *action based on prejudice*. In this section, we will briefly take a look at what goes wrong and how to begin to put it right.

One of the very first things that we learn in life for our survival is to discriminate between what nourishes us and what threatens us. The act of discriminating is a healthy and essential constructive process. For example, with emergent strategy it is important to be able to discriminate between totally wacky ideas and those that hold some potential.

However, human nature being what it is, discrimination can also become locked into a destructive process, as shown in Figure 15.4.

This illustration also indicates the types of interventions that are useful in each part of the cycle to change the destructive process which builds up. The following definitions taken from *Collins English Dictionary* are also helpful in pulling together a common understanding in this area:

... sustainable change means offering a supportive environment where people can discover their polarities ... without recrimination. Clayton and Bentley (1996)

Stereotyped   Lacking originality or individuality
Stereotyping   An idea, trait or convention that has grown stale through fixed usage
Assumption   The act of taking something for granted

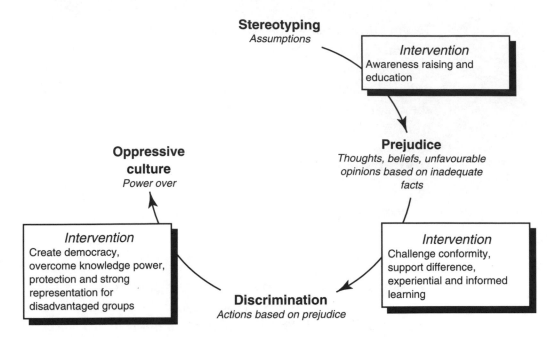

FIGURE 15.4 The process of destructive discrimination

Prejudice   An opinion formed beforehand, especially an unfavourable one based on inadequate facts

The reason why this area is so important to emergent strategy is that our sticky stereotyping and fixed prejudices get in the way of discovering novelty, and from seeing multiple realities.

STEREOTYPING

Stereotyping is a healthy and useful process because it creates stability. It means that every time we go out of the door in the morning we do not have to go through a lengthy process of making sense of the world from scratch. We can build on past information, knowledge and experiences. The trouble is we get lazy, we rely too much on our ability to do this and consequently do not spend enough time checking out the assumptions which exist within our stereotyping – we allow these assumptions to travel too deep, without question, into our understanding of the world. This leads to some solidifying of our view of the world.

Checking your stereotyping process is to become aware

of the assumptions that you make about people and situations, continuously updating your repertoire of knowledge.

PREJUDICE AND DISCRIMINATION
As solidifying increases, so prejudices begin to form. Prejudices can be very destructive for ourselves and others. If we use our prejudices as part of our discriminating process, that is when discrimination becomes locked into fixed, destructive cycles.

When you hold a prejudice you will tend to see only the behaviours or the attributes which support your beliefs. Prejudice is not confined to people alone. For example, you might hold a prejudice towards a system, like an organization's competency system, which in the past was damaging for you. In this case, you would be generalizing your negative belief to encompass *all* competency systems and so your prejudice begins; setting up a reinforcing feedback system, rather than one that challenges your belief. You will then discriminate; that is, act and behave on the basis of your prejudice.

Prejudice does not necessarily arise from direct experience. For example, where significant people in our lives hold and show prejudice we can pick them up. The media, too, have a lot to answer for in their contributions to generating prejudice. Children are especially vulnerable to this, often holding their beliefs without challenging them in their adult lives.

Often the undoing of prejudice and negative discrimination is simply achieved through recognizing what you are doing; that is, to become aware of and own your prejudices. Sometimes it is more difficult because the undoing reveals truths that are painful. I have seen this in broken relationships and fragmented groups where one or both parties have become prejudiced towards the other. The pain has been in realizing the loss, and owning that 'I/we' actually contributed to the problem in the first place and that it wasn't/isn't 'all their fault'.

Discrimination based on prejudice leads to an imbalance of power out of which grows oppression. The following exercise offers a process for bringing to the surface assumptions and beliefs related to stereotyping and prejudices.

Exercise 47 – Team awareness

For this exercise you will need a set of blank cards and some pens.

Using the blank cards, each team member must write on a card:

1. The name of another member of the team.
2. An assumption they make about that team member.
3. A prejudice that they have towards that team member.

An example is shown in Figure 15.5.

Each team member then collects up the cards from their team about themselves. Allow time for everyone to consider what has been said on their cards, then give each team member up to five minutes to respond.

Your role as their manager will be to hold the fact that while statements may be *true* or *false*, they in fact say as much about the giver as the receiver. The recipient should become aware of any patterns in the messages on the cards.

For example

To:	Simon
From:	Anonymous
Date:	15 August
Assumption:	I think that your very fixed outcome-oriented approach actually narrows opportunities for you.
Prejudice:	I believe that the area where you were brought up, makes you more likely to be aggressive than others here.

FIGURE 15.5 Prejudice card

This is an exercise which could be repeated on a regular basis, each time adding some value to your team's understanding of each other and to the team's strategic thinking.

SUMMARY

Valuing and appreciating that people bring their difference to the work place and making efforts to discover different thoughts and ideas, will add to the rich tapestry available to you for developing strategy. Building positive feedback systems which support this process will sustain both a sense of belonging and a willingness to reveal difference.

You are, however, faced with a dilemma – the act of conforming reduces many anxieties; in a sense it keeps the lid on some of the more uncomfortable and difficult issues that tend to float around organizations. Yet in this act, novelty, an important aspect of emergent strategy, is lost. In order to bring novelty into the work place management and staff will have to begin to uncover and deal with those issues that people manage to hide in the conforming culture. In so doing they will also bring people to the boundary of their learning.

CHAPTER 16

DEVELOPING INTEGRATED STRATEGY

KEY LEARNING POINTS

- Understand the true integration of emergent and determined strategy
- Know how to integrate these two different approaches for developing strategy

What is integrated strategy? What does it look like? How can an integrated way of operating be better than the approach that you are already using? There are no simple answers to these questions because there is no *one* way.

It is likely that in some ways you are already using an integrated approach to developing strategy. Speak to any top manager and they will probably tell you the same. Yet, what you see is determined strategy. What you haven't seen is integrated or emergent strategy, because until recently neither have been well defined in the business arena.

The difference between current practices and new ways of working in the future, is whether you trust to luck, or whether you develop integrated strategy through conscious awareness. Practising strategy integration with awareness can begin in small steps – in a team project, or in a personal project like my example below, as well as at an organizational level.

A personal project

Writing this book has in many ways been a co-created process; not just in my writing but also through my network of colleagues and friends who have often shifted my thinking through discussion and consultation.

I worked with both an emergent and determined approach – emergent in formulating learning processes to support the theory; determined in structuring each section and chapter into a cohesive whole.

For practising strategy development at an organizational level you might like to refer back to Chapter 6, where you assessed the conditions of your organization and related your team's thinking styles to those conditions. In working through this book things may have changed for you and your team. You might like to plot your different styles again, using Figure 16.1, in the light of learning and changes since you started.

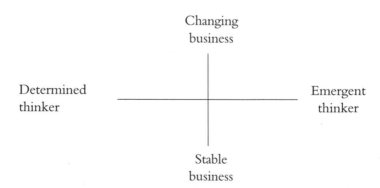

FIGURE 16.1 Linking organizational change and personal style

DEVELOPING AN INTEGRATED APPROACH

In Chapter 2 I suggested that strategic thinking is a journey. That is, a journey without a clear destination. Clear destinations are rarely achieved in long-term strategy. The importance lies in the journey; a journey on two feet, one emergent, the other determined. Stay on one foot too long and your journey stops. The two feet are symbolic of integration, no longer an either/or, the choice is both/and:

Stay on one foot too long and your journey stops

- *both* structure *and* flexibility
- *both* intention *and* learning
- *both* head *and* heart
- *both* known *and* unknown
- *both* control *and* order.

The choice is not 'either/ or'. The choice is 'both/ and'. Stacey (1993)

Integration means 'the act of combining or adding parts to make a unified whole'. You can only achieve a unified whole through awareness and choice.

Take, for instance, one of the examples from the list above 'known and unknown'. How could you integrate both known and unknown into developing an integrated strategy? If you think about it, determined strategy is more about working with the known and emergent strategy is more about working with the unknown; so you would:

- Develop structured forms of control to handle the *knowable*.
- Build on self-organizing forms of patterns and order to handle the *unknowable*.

Let's look at this idea using the scenario of the restaurant.

Scenario – A new strategy for the restaurant

Caroline and Mark decided that they would develop their new strategy for the business using an integrated approach. They already had the support of the staff through their efforts in building good staff relations over the period following Henry's death. This was important because change initiatives work better if people feel supported – if nothing else there was good mutual support and respect within the staff team. On top of this, Caroline and Mark were completely open about their naivety in running a business, and showed their willingness to learn.

At a staff meeting three months after the funeral, Caroline and Mark discussed with the staff how they would like to develop a new strategy for the business. They explained what this meant using some examples.

They had already established a common purpose with the staff two weeks earlier: *To run the finest restaurant in the region, renowned for its good food and family atmosphere.*

Caroline and Mark were clear about some values for themselves:

- The enjoyment of work and health of the staff
- Involvement of staff in the business.

They were less clear about what a set of common values for all the staff would be. They offered some ideas:

- Customers are important
- Variety of food on the menu with regular changes on specialities
- Serving the local community.

Then suggested that everyone think about what might be important for them as a staff team.

They felt that they were unable to define a long-term vision and were happy to develop a strategy to fulfil the defined purpose. Some areas they were clear about; others they were less clear about. Areas which they were able to define (knowable) included:

- Health and safety (to explore different ways of achieving high standards required)
- Employment contracts
- Management of staff

> Some of the most effective strategies we uncovered in our research combined deliberation and control with flexibility and organizational learning.
> Mintzberg (1987)

- Finance and budgeting
- Information from their S.W.O.T. analysis
- Staff views on what key success factors might be for the business and what limiting factors existed.

These were all related to a deterministic approach.

Areas which they were less clear about (unknowable) included:

- Purchasing (Caroline and Mark wanted to raise the standards of their purchasing but didn't quite know what to do about this)
- Marketing – developing a new image
- Staff development
- Specialities and menu items
- Customer needs
- How to make the customer feel welcome
- Lay out of the restaurant
- Special events
- Other areas which were less defined.

These would all be developed through an emergent approach.

The fact that Caroline and Mark were clear about the way they wanted to work enabled them to establish enough controls without being too controlling, and some points of reference to enable the formation of new ideas and initiatives without becoming too chaotic.

HOLDING A POINT OF REFERENCE

A point of reference is a form of control; a map for the journey, where everyone is following the same map. Margaret Wheatley says 'Meaning and purpose serve as a point of reference'. In any organization, however large or small, where there is common purpose there is always a point of reference, out of which order is created. With common purpose, determined and emergent strategy can weave in and around each other; they can become integrated.

Commonly held values and clear boundaries also act as points of reference.

MARKING THE BOUNDARIES

Chaos is bounded instability, we therefore have to look for the boundaries. Stacey (1992)

Boundaries create limits or define specific changes perceived to be necessary for the success of the business. They come to the strategist in two categories – 'What' and 'How'.

'What' boundaries are usually very clear, being laid down in such terms as productivity, finance and sales.

For example

'Costs will be cut by 10 per cent in the next 12 months through increased efficiency'

This example was proposed by a group of senior managers. The statement determined the boundary, allowing people lower down the organization to work with an emergent approach within it. Mintzberg referred to this type of top-down strategy development as the 'Umbrella strategy'.

'How' boundaries are less clear and likely to exist in policy, procedures and cultural behaviour. Certain boundaries are controlled, within which emergent strategy then operates.

For example

Some procedures of organizational functioning, such as staffing policies and quality systems, are controlled through a deterministic approach; while the content of the work is self organizing around these controls. Both management and staff are involved with strategy development; management using a deterministic approach to establish and maintain the controls, then all management and staff following an emergent approach for the content of the work.

Both *What* and *How* boundaries for the development of integrated strategy have been operating for a number of years in organizations requiring creativity and specialist expertise. Mintzberg points out that in such cases implementors of the strategy also need to be formulators of the strategy, simply because it is people with the technical know-how who understand the products. The specialist or technician also become the strategists.

SUMMARY

And so in the end is your beginning; the specialist is the strategist; the child is the strategist; we all have the potential to be strategists.

Scenario – The success of the restaurant

Caroline and Mark discovered the strategists in their staff. Not only did they survive, they became a very successful enterprise.

It turned out that one of the waitresses had an interest in wine – that is, 'knowledge' rather than excess drinking! Mark and Caroline supported her development in this area, which she then passed on to the rest of the staff. The restaurant became known for its excellent wine cellar in both variety and value for money. The staff impressed customers with their knowledge of wine, and the good advice offered to complement the excellent menu. Caroline and Mark could never have envisaged this in their early days of taking over the business.

They weren't without their setbacks at times, but they were able to survive uncertainty and to ride the ebb and flow of business life without too much stress, due to the commitment and innovation of their staff.

Developing strategy means deciding how you want to travel on your journey, and to know the boundaries and limits of your map. Above all you need to have a desire for adventure, to learn, to take risks and to discover new dimensions in the terrain through which you travel.

Your journey starts now.

APPENDIX

SOLUTION TO PART OF EXERCISE 14

One solution to this puzzle is to think of the phrase 'six letters' not numerically but as two words 'six' and 'letters'. When these two words are crossed out, the word **BANANA** remains.

A second solution is to eliminate *all* incidences of the *first six letters*. The first six letters are B S A I N C X; A N and S occur twice. When they are removed the word **LETTER** remains.

This exercise demonstrates an important lesson. Generally people stop when they find an answer to a puzzle. Creativity demands more . . . you must keep looking for additional answers and solutions.

REFERENCES

Clarkson, P. and Mackewn, J., *Fritz Perls: Key Figures in Counselling and Psychotherapy*, Sage, 1995.

Clayton, S. and Bentley, T., 'Gestalt – a philosophy for change: Integrating extremes', *Training Officer*, **32** (5), 1996.

Garrett, B., *Learning to Lead*, Harper Collins, 1991.

Garrett, B., 'Helicopters and rotting fish', in *Developing Strategy*, Garrett, B. (ed.), McGraw-Hill, 1995.

Hanford, P., 'Developing director and executive competencies in strategic thinking', in *Developing Strategic Thought*, Garrett, B. (ed.), McGraw-Hill, 1995.

Johnson, I. and Scholes, K., *Exploring Corporate Strategy*, Prentice-Hall, 1988.

Mintzberg, H., 'Crafting strategy', *Harvard Business Review*, July–August, 1987.

Mintzberg, H. and Waters, J.A., 'Of strategies deliberate and emergent', *Strategic Management Journal*, **6**, pp. 257–72, 1985.

Ohmae, K. *The Mind of the Strategist*, Penguin, 1982.

Pascale, R. *Managing on the Edge*, Penguin, 1990.

Roddick, A., *Body and Soul*, Vermillion, 1992.

Senge, P., *The Fifth Discipline: The Art and Practice of the Learning Organization*, Century, 1990.

Springer, S.P. and Deutsch, G., *Left Brain, Right Brain*, W.H. Freeman & Company, 1981.

Stacey, R., *Managing Chaos: Dynamic Business Strategies in an Unpredictable World*, Kogan Page, 1992.

Stacey, R., 'Strategy as order emerging from chaos', *Long Range Planning*, **26** (1), pp. 10–17, 1993.

Sworder, C., 'Hearing the baby's cry: it's all in the thinking', in *Developing Strategic Thought*, Garrett, B. (ed.), McGraw-Hill, 1995.

Wheatley, M.J., *Leadership and the New Science*, Berrett-Koehler, 1992.

INDEX